GREAT WINES UNDER $20

ELYSE LURAY

Published by

Krause Publications, a division of F+W Media, Inc.
700 East State Street • Iola, WI 54990-0001
715-445-2214 • 888-457-2873
www.krausebooks.com

To order books or other products call toll-free 1-800-258-0929
or visit us online at www.krausebooks.com or www.Shop.Collect.com

Cover photography by Shannon Stapleton

ISBN-13: 978-1-4402-1448-6
ISBN-10: 1-4402-1448-4

Cover Design by Frank Rivera
Interior Design by Heidi Bittner-Zastrow
Edited by Mark Moran

Printed in China

Contents

I am a pop-culture girl...

My idea of buying an affordable bottle of wine is to spend $20 or less, and "less" is an important component. This book was inspired by the frustration that I experienced as the result of being a wine auctioneer. I was selling wines for substantial and sometimes astronomical sums. Occasionally, I was invited to try them and learned to love wine.

My dilemma? Buying wines to drink or serve to my friends at a price that I could afford. So I began an organized search for wines of all types, that were affordable, yet provided quality and enjoyment. The result is this book, which is designed to share the wines I discovered, offer insights into how they were found and encourage others to begin their own quests.

I am a pop-culture girl. After graduating from Tulane University, I spent 11 years at Christie's auction house appraising memorabilia and 20th-century items, and eventually became a Vice President and Director of the Collectibles and Popular Culture Department. During my career as an auctioneer, I had sold almost every category that Christie's handles—except wine. So you can imagine my trepidation when I was invited to sell for Zachys Wine Auctions.

Some of Zachys auctions are held in New York City and typically the value of the wines averages more than $1,000 per lot. Although I've always believed a good auctioneer does not need to be an expert in what they are selling, I faced some challenges. First problem: I could

An inviting spread at the Setriolo Vineyards near Chianti, Italy.

not pronounce anything. Second problem: I knew nothing about wine. Lastly, I simply could not afford to start buying the high-priced wines I was selling.

So, with the help of the gracious staff at Zachys, I set out to learn about wine. I had to learn proper pronunciations, especially for all of the foreign brands. Jeff Zacharia of Zachys recorded auctioneer Fritz Hatton in action. I spent the next three months listening to Fritz, pronouncing wine names in my car as I drove carpool for my two boys and their friends.

However, I still needed to learn much more about wine. So I took the same approach used in my investigations as a *History Detective* on the PBS program. Wine, like any object, has history, culture, geographic influences, comparables in the marketplace and certainly a huge amount of literature. I soon realized that learning the history of wine was not my biggest challenge.

The difficult part began when I went into a wine store to shop for myself. I was completely overwhelmed. I was a novice learning the trade, but I wanted to drink good wines and not go broke in the process.

This book is the result of my journey into learning about wines and, in the process, discovering as many as I could that I love and can afford. I applied my *History Detectives* techniques to learn about wine and so can you! In this book, you'll find everything I learned along the way: demystifying stemware, wine language, food pairings and more. I do not profess to be anywhere near a wine expert, but I know now that you do not need to be in order to enjoy great wine. And most importantly, I know now that I can afford to drink good—and sometimes great—wine and have fun long the way without breaking the bank! After reading the book, I hope you do, too.

I'd love to hear from you if you have any comments, wine suggestions or other thoughts. You can contact me at www.Elyseluray.com.

Cheers! Salute! L'Chaim! Kampai! Oogy wawa! A Votre Sante!

How to Read a Label

Before I started to investigate wines for this book, I must admit that the attractiveness of the label was often a major influence on my purchases. If the label caught my attention, I was more likely to reach for it than another bottle. Sure, artwork and packaging are key, but I quickly learned that the labels are an important source of information and can help to select a wine more to your taste. From my experience on *History Detectives* and my earlier career at Christie's Auctioneers, I find that wine labels remind me of the kind of documents often found in an archive, and like old documents, there is plenty to be learned from them.

Photo by Shannon Stapleton

CHATEAU
LABOURÉ-ROI

BOURGOGNE
BLANC
CHARDONNAY

APPELLATION BOURGOGNE CONTRÔLÉE

ÉLEVÉ ET MIS EN BOUTEILLE AU CHÂTEAU
Château Labouré-Roi, Récoltant à Meursault, Côte d'Or
PRODUIT DE FRANCE

Here is the information usually available on the label. By the way, information on the front of a wine label is regulated by the U.S. Alcohol and Tobacco Tax and Trade Bureau.

Besides the brand name, you'll find:

> **Type:** chardonnay, red, table … What is it?
> **Vintage:** year produced
> **Alcohol:** content by volume—"acl/vol"
> **Size of bottle:** usually 1,500, 750, 500 or 350 ml
> **Vineyard:** often a family name, region name, etc
> **Country of origin**
> **Bottler:** name and location

Phrases like "Contains Sulfites" and health warnings will appear as a government requirement.

There are confusing aspects when trying to determine from a label where the wine was bottled and produced. Basically if the words "bottled by" are on the label, then the wine was produced somewhere else. If the label says "Produced and Bottled by," then it means that no less then 75% of the wine was produced by the bottler. (If you like the wine, do not concern yourself with this. I am just pointing it just out so you know the difference.)

A listing of the wine's alcohol content is required by law on the bottle. If the wine is more then 14% alcohol — or "fortified" — then the tax may be higher. Imported wines must include the name of the importer.

Often there is another label, or the back, with the brand name. It may include some of the required information, as well as a brief description or promotional verbiage designed to entice you to purchase this particular product.

On the Question of Corks ...

Since I began investigating wines under $20 for this book, one of the interesting things that I learned is that more wine bottles now come with a screw cap rather than a cork, and many "corks" are now made of plastic! Which is better?

First, a little history. Corks have been used as bottle stoppers for as long as we have had wine. Research shows corks were used by ancient Greeks and Romans, and corks begin to appear in literature as early at the 16th century. A hundred years later, glass bottles were developed having almost a standard diameter opening, thus making the cork a top choice for sealing the bottle. As a result, glass bottles and cork stoppers helped to standardize the wine trade. Wines could now be shipped greater distances, warehoused and stored for longer periods.

Cork failing, also known as cork taint or corked wine, is the chemical reaction that causes the wine to spoil. Wine aficionados claim that there has been a decrease in this problem in the last five years.

Most of the wines featured in this book are produced with the idea that they will be consumed within a few years—aging is not part of the process. When you open one of these bottles you should not have to worry about feeling the cork or sniffing the wine, as many wine lovers do, although it can be a wonderful part of the ritual of enjoying wine. And it's important to note that many experts believe the cork reveals nothing about a wine's quality.

The most common cork alternatives are Cellukork, a plastic substance, and the simple crew cap. Cellukork looks like a real cork and a corkscrew is still required to open the bottle.

And the screw cap? It tends to be more common on economical wines than those that are higher priced, but this is not a hard and fast rule. There are wines that exceed the parameters of this book —selling for than $20 per bottle—that are now using the screw cap. There seems to be a question as to whether or not the wine can age properly over a period of time.

I love the screw cap! It is easy to open, makes the wine easy to save and you don't have to worry about carrying around a corkscrew, if you're on a picnic, for example, or traveling by air. Some wine producers must agree with me, as the use of screw caps is estimated to be increasing by 500 million bottles annually worldwide (see *winecurmudgeon.com*).

On the other hand, there are many who love using a corkscrew. Some find it romantic, others need the ritual, but they all love the old-school way of opening a bottle of wine containing a cork. I say, to each his own and just enjoy the wine!

Wine bottle stoppers/closures include (from left) screw caps, traditional cork, Cellukork and a cap/cork combination.

Glasses

Does the glass you use to drink wine matter? I think so.

Wine collectors often have different glasses for the wines they drink. While many of us only have a single style of wine glass that we use for both reds and whites, you can enhance your enjoyment by having both red- and white-wine glasses.

Chardonnay-style, white-wine glasses and Bordeaux-style, red-wine glasses are more than sufficient. If you are confused as to which glass to use, the general rule is a smaller, narrower glass —preferably a tulip shape—for white wines, and a wider, larger-rimmed glass for the reds. Smaller surfaces prevent warming in white wines and larger surfaces allow for more development of the favors and aromas in red wines. If you can only afford one style, buy the Bordeaux.

You may have noticed that wine glasses without stems are on the market and growing in popularity. Do you need a stem? It's a personal choice, but I like and recommend them. The stem allows you to hold the glass without heat from your hand warming the wine. Some wine lovers will never go back after using glasses without stems, while others will never accept them. It really is a personal preference, so try both and make your choice.

(I must admit that some of my wine tasting was done while at the beach where only plastic cups were available. I can state emphatically that plastic cups do not allow for full enjoyment of the wine!)

Wine glasses are available in a wide range of prices, but you do not have to spend a lot of money on them. I bought mine at Costco and Home Goods. I also have rather expensive crystal Waterford glasses, which I love to use and they look beautiful on my table, but they do not make wine purchased for $20 or less taste any better.

Photos by André Karwath, Wikipedia

What Vintage Should I Drink?

Vintage is the year the wine is produced and this will appear on the front label of the bottle. Should you care? Probably not when you are drinking young and/or inexpensive wines. Each wine that I've discovered as a result of my "sleuthing" is ready to drink now or in the next year or two.

It is a common mistake to think that almost all wines improve with age. Only a select few actually do and these are usually more expensive. For the purposes of this book, I am not focusing on the vintages of the wines. If there is a vintage year on the label illustrated, it is the bottle that we drank for our wine tasting.

For the most part, inexpensive wines are best consumed by their second or third year, including the red wines. At our target price point, the vintage dates can serve as a "freshness" guide. If you see two vintages on the shelf, take the more recent.

It is important to remember that the vintage date year tells us two things: the age of the wine and whether or not the wine was produced in a "good" year. Several factors are involved, but usually, the better the climate conditions in a given year, the better the production of the wine, and thus, it's usually more expensive and collectible. Taste may vary slightly, but for the most part, at this price point, the taste stays the same.

If you want to delve deeper into wine culture, you can use vintages to add another variable in selecting wines, regardless of price, and try to obtain the best years for those that you choose. Keep this in mind, if only to enhance your wine experience.

What Food Should I Pair Wine With?

I always say: With art, go with your own taste, don't listen to others. I believe it's the same with wine and food, but after much research and tasting, there are some tips that I can share.

"White wine with fish and red wine with meat" is the one I came across the most. While this rule is not written in stone, it does have some validity.

You usually cannot go wrong when pairing food and wine by region.

The wine shouldn't overpower the food, and the food should not overwhelm the wine. Balance the flavor of the wine with the food. Pair light-bodied wines with lighter dishes and full-bodied wines with more intense flavors and richer meals.

Here are some wine/food suggestion:

REDS

Cabernet Sauvignon: Best with rich or intense-flavored food. Grilled meats, lamb, pot roast, Italian cuisine, Chinese (meats) and heavy cheeses, like brie, camembert, strong cheddar.

Merlot: This wine can be paired with mild to rich-flavored food. It goes well with a grilled salmon but can also be paired with turkey, lamb chops, and Italian cuisine. Some like it with Chinese dishes, as well.

Pinot Noir: This light-bodied wine goes great with grilled seafood, smoky dishes like barbeque, bacon, and ribs. You can also try the wine with light pastas, and even a baked ham.

Syrah/Shiraz: This spicy wine goes well with casual food, including pizza, pastas, sausages, fajitas, burritos, and barbeque. It also pairs well with grilled seafood.

Malbec: This semi-spicy wine pairs well with Italian cuisine, pizza, steak, all grilled meats, Mediterranean foods and sauces, as well as other intense flavors.

Zinfandel: This spicy wine pairs well with more intense flavors, including Italian, barbeque, grilled seafood, pizza, burgers, pastas, and grilled meats.

WHITES

Chardonnay: Pairs well with rich food, and creamy sauces and butter. Excellent with seafood (including shellfish), veal, and chicken. Great with mild and strong cheeses.

Riesling (Dry): Goes well with a mix of summer foods including shellfish and oysters, and some Italian foods like veal piccata and chicken marsala. It also goes well during cocktail hour, when serving dried fruits, salsa, and nuts.

Riesling (Sweet): This sweet wine lends itself to Thai, Chinese, Asian, and Indian dishes. Smoked fish works well and it can be good with Cheshire, Colby, edam, gouda, and Monterey Jack cheeses.

Pinot Gris/Pinot Grigio: This light- to medium-bodied wine is excellent with grilled seafood, Mediterranean and Italian cuisine, Tex-Mex, and Asian dishes. Pairs well with Parmesan cheese.

Sauvignon Blanc: This wine is always good with seafood (including shellfish), snapper, trout, raw oysters, sushi, halibut, and tuna. Caesar salad, mild cheeses, and Mexican and Asian food also pair well.

Viognier: This light, crisp wine lends itself to seafood including lobster, scallops, and shrimp. It also pairs well with cream-based noodle sauces.

Food Pairing Icons

Meat
(Beef, lamb, roasts, pork chops, meatloaf)

Poultry
(Chicken, turkey, duck)

Casual foods
(Hamburgers, hot dogs, chili, pizza)

Fish and seafood

Asian cuisine

Spicy foods

Cheese

Salads

Grilled foods
(Meats, vegetables, veggie burgers)

Fruits and Nuts

Italian and Mediterranean cuisine

Just Chill ... Or Not

Serving wine can be confusing. With most beverages, we know which are served better hot—like coffee—or cold—like lemonade. With wine, it varies. Here are some guidelines, but as with tasting wine, this is a personal choice.

Red wine is routinely served at room temperature and white wine is served cold. "Room temperature" really means somewhere between 50 to 55 degrees Fahrenheit, but most of us do not keep our homes that cold. Room temperature is defined as what a wine cellar environment should be. The term was coined centuries ago when the "room" was in a stone building with no heating, air conditioning or humidifiers. For white wine, most people store their bottles in the refrigerator. That's fine, but this may be too cold for maximum enjoyment. To compensate, take it out 20 minutes before you serve it. Here are some recommendations:

Most Whites: 43 to 53 F
Full-Bodied Whites: 50 to 55 F
Light Reds: 50 to 60 F
Medium-Bodied Reds: 55 to 65 F
Bold Reds: 62 to 67 F

Sometimes, with red wine especially, you may notice that your first sip is quite different from the taste 10 minutes later. It usually means that the wine needed to "breathe." Letting a bottle breathe simply means exposing the wine to air. The oxygen helps the wine soften or loosen its tannins (the diverse group of chemical compounds in wine that can affect the color, aging ability, and texture). Most, but not all, of the wines in this book do not need to breathe, as they do not require any further aging. Most whites and rosés do not need to breathe at all.

If you think your chosen wine needs to breathe, keep it in your glass for a while or pour it into a decanter. Uncorking the bottle is not enough, as the neck of the bottle is too small to let much air inside. Most importantly, sit back, relax, and enjoy your wine!

Types of Red Wine

Barbera: A red grape common in the Piedmont region of north-western Italy.
Main growing regions: Piedmont and Lombardy, Italy; California.
Body: medium to full.
Tasting notes: "grapey," easy to drink.

Cabernet Sauvignon: Probably the most notable of red wines with its big, complex, and powerful flavors. Some call it the "King of Reds."
Main growing regions: Bordeaux, Australia, California, Washington State, Chile, Tuscany.
Body: medium to full.
Tasting notes: black currant, green or bell pepper, chocolate, mint, and spice flavors.

Grenache: A grape grown primarily in the Rhône Valley.
Main growing regions: Spain, Rhône Valley, and California.
Body: medium to full.
Tasting Notes: sweet, raspberry, fruit flavors.

Malbec: a red grape known for its popularity in Argentina.
Main growing regions: Argentina, Bordeaux.
Body: medium to full.
Tasting notes: spicy, raspberry, chocolate.

Merlot: Easy-drinking red wine. Third-most-planted grape in France. (Sometimes called "drink it now," meaning the wine was not produced to be stored for a long period of time. All the wines in this book are "drink it now," but some may have a longer shelf life.)
Main growing regions: Bordeaux, Australia, California, Washington State, Chile, Northern Italy, and New York's Long Island.
Body: medium.

Tasting notes: plums, currants, blackberries, mocha, and black cherry.

Pinot Noir: Known for its growth in Burgundy and the northwestern United States, this wine is hard to grow but produces a wonderful light wine for all occasions.
Main growing regions: Burgundy, California, and Oregon.
Body: light to medium.
Tasting notes: Cherry, raspberries, soil, cola, and smoke.

Sangiovese: Primary grape in Chianti, grown primarily in Tuscany. Good to drink early and very affordable.
Main growing regions: Tuscany, some California.
Body: light to medium.
Tasting notes: Cherries and raisins.

Syrah/Shiraz: Called Shiraz in Australia, but everywhere else in the world the wine is known as Syrah.
Main growing regions: Rhône Valley, Australia, and California.
Body: medium.
Tasting notes: plums, spices, blackberry, and blueberry.

Tempranillo: Spain's answer to Cabernet Sauvignon, major grape of Spain.
Main growing region: Rioja, Spain.
Body: Light to medium.
Tasting notes: cherry, spicy, and smoky.

Zinfandel: The all-American grape!
Main growing region: California.
Body: medium to full.
Tasting notes: berry, spicy, blackberry, and black pepper.

Types of White Wine

Chardonnay: A white grape, grown primarily in Burgundy, France.
Main growing regions: Burgundy, California, Oregon, Washington State, Australia, New Zealand, South Africa, and Chile.
Body: light to medium.
Tasting notes: can vary, but often buttery, vanilla, fruits, toast, nuts, and oak.

Chenin Blanc: A white grape known mostly in the Loire Valley of France.
Main growing regions: Loire, California, New Zealand, and South Africa.
Body: light to medium.
Tasting notes: melon, honey—very soft, light.

Pinot Grigo/Pinot Gris: A white grape that Italians call Pinot Grigio and French call Pinot Gris.
Main growing regions: Italy, Alsace, Oregon, and California.
Body: medium to full.
Tasting notes: softer, orange, fruity.

Riesling: A white grape, which originated in the Rhine region of Germany.
Main growing regions: Germany, Austria, Alsace (France), Washington, and New York Finger Lakes Region. There are also significant plantings in Luxembourg, northern Italy, Australia, New Zealand, South Africa, China, and Ukraine.
Body: Light to medium.
Tasting notes: sweet, citrus, and fruity.

Sauternes: French dessert wine, made from Sémillon, Sauvignon Blanc, and Muscadelle grapes that have been affected by *Botrytis cinerea*, also known as "noble rot." This causes the grapes to become partially "raisined," resulting in concentrated and distinctively flavored wines.
Main growing region: the Sauternais region of the Graves section in Bordeaux.
Body: full.
Tasting notes: apricot, honey, and peach.

Sauvignon Blanc: A white grape, usually a crisp and tart wine.
Main growing regions: Bordeaux, Loire, California, New Zealand, and South Africa.
Body: light to medium.
Tasting notes: herbs, melons, gooseberry, and grapefruit.

Viognier: a white wine grape. It is the only permitted grape for the French wine Condrieu in the Rhône Valley.
Main growing regions: Rhône Valley and California.
Body: medium to full.
Tasting notes: peach, apricot, and fruity.
Standard food pairings: seafood, shellfish, and some chicken and pork.

Elyse and winemaker Susanna in the barrel room at Setriolo Vineyards near Chianti, Italy.

Wine-Growing Regions

Argentina

The foothills of the Andes Mountains are perfect for vineyards. Malbec has clearly become the grape of choice. Medoza is Argentina's largest and best wine-producing region and is the country's center for winemaking today. Other grapes that perform well are Cabernet, Merlot, and Chardonnay.

Australia

Australia is probably best known for Shiraz, the Aussie name for Syrah, and is made from big and oaky to light and refreshing. There are 50 regions and sub-regions throughout the country. The Barossa Valley (known for Rieslings, Shiraz and Cabernet Sauvignon), Coonawara, Yarra Valley, and Hunter Valley are also popular.

Chile

Becoming well known for good but inexpensive wines. Many Chilean wineries now proudly bottle Carménère. Some of the popular regions are Casablanca, Maipo, Rapel, and Colchagua Province.

France

Many believe the French set the winemaking standard for the rest of the world.

The best way to understand the wines is to break them down into seven major regions: Bordeaux, Burgundy, Rhône, Loire, Alsace, Languedoc, and Champagne.

Bordeaux: An industrial city in southwestern France, it is the center of the world's most famous wine region. Wine estates here are called chateaus.

The region is known for: Dry white wines, which include blends of Sauvignon Blanc and Semillon. Sweet dessert wines encompass blends of Sauvignon Blanc, Semillon, and Muscadelle afflicted with *Botrytis cinerea* ("noble rot"). Medium-bodied red wines comprise blends of Cabernet Sauvignon, Merlot, Cabernet Franc, Malbec and Petit Verdot.

Some sub-regions produce wine made primarily from Cabernet Sauvignon, whereas the Merlot grape is dominant in other areas.

Sub-regions of the Bordeaux include Graves (dry wines and Cabernet reds), Entre-Deux-Mers (light and simple whites), Médoc (Cabernet reds), Sauternes (sweet dessert wines) and Saint-Emilion (Merlot reds, blended with a significant amount of Cabernet Franc)

Burgundy: In this region, many small growers can make up one vineyard. Most red wines are made from the Pinot Noir grape, while in the southern part—Beaujolais—the Gamay grape is used. White wines are predominately made with Chardonnay.

The sub-regions of Burgundy include Chablis (very dry white wines), Côte de Nuits (full-bodied reds), Côte de Beaune (light Pinot Noir and great whites, especially Chardonnay), Côte Chalonnaise (less-expensive reds and whites), Mâcon (excellent whites including Pouilly-Fuissé) and Beaujolais (known for its Gamay production).

Rhône: South of the Burgundy region is the Rhône River Valley, known for its earthy, gutsy wines, both red and white. Northern Rhône reds—including Syrah-based—are from Côte Rotie, Crozes-Hermitage, Cornas, and St Joseph. Whites are based on the Viognier grape or a blend of Marsanne. In the southern region of Rhône, the wines are mainly produced with Grenache grapes.

Loire: Known for its white wines including Muscadet, Vouray, Rosé, Pouilly-Fumé and Sancerre.

The quality of the wine is controlled by the government.

AOC—Appellation d'Origine Contrôlée: The most widely applied standard used on French wine labels, indicating the wine meets the legal requirements for the area designated. The more specific the area of origin, the higher the standards.

VDQS—Vin Délimité de Qualité Supérieure: This is the second set of standards used for wines in areas not covered by the AOC laws. Although the wines labeled as such are a notch lower in quality, VDQS is still a reliable government guarantee.

Vin de Pays: This is the third set, slightly more relaxed, used to regulate "country wines" The phrase is always followed by a region.

Italy

Italians produce and drink more wine than any other country. I recently returned from my first trip to Tuscany and noticed that everywhere you go you see grapes growing. In Italy, most of these grapes are Barbera, Dolcetto, Nebbiolo, and Sangiovese.

Italian labels can be a bit confusing. When you read the label, you will notice the location of the vineyard is how they name their wines, similar to France. For example, Chianti is a winemaking area and the grape most likely used is the Sangiovese grape, although most labels read Chianti.

Italy has 20 wine-growing regions: Calabria, Apulia, Basilicata, Campania, Molise, Abruzzo, Latium, Umbria, Marche, Tuscany, Emilia-Romagna, Liguira, Piedmont, Valle d'Aosta, Lombardy, Trentino-Alto-Adige, Veneto and Friuli-Venezia Giulia, plus the islands of Sicily and Sardinia.

In this book, you will find wines from some of these regions, including:

Campania: In southern Italy, the main grape of the region is Aglianico and can produce quite expensive wines.

Tuscany: The Chianti region is one of the most prolific and produces some incredible wine for the price. The area is divided into seven zones: Classico, Colli Senesi, Rufina, Colli Aretini, Colline Pisane, Collie Fiorentini, and Montalbano.

Also selected for this book are wines from the Montepulciano region, known as Vino Nobile de Montepulciano. This rich wine is Sangiovese-based. Another wine is the Rosso di Montalcino, which is based on the Brunello grape and known as a light-bodied and inexpensive wine.

Veneto: A northern region that produces a diverse amount of wines, including Amarone Barolino, Soave, Prosecco, Valpolicella, and many varietals. A blend of the Garganega grape is widely used for Soave whites, and a blend of the Corvina grape is used for Valpolicella wines.

Piedmont: Piedmont is the region that some say produces the finest wines, such as Barbera, Barolo, Barbaresco, Fresisa, Dolcetto, Nebbiolo, Gavi, Grignolino, Malvasia and Asti Spumante, among others. The main grape grown here is the Nebbiolo and is the foundation for Barolo and Barbersso. Included in this book are wines made of Nebbiolo and Barbera.

As in France, Italian wine quality is controlled by the government. You will notice the following categories on Italian wine labels:

DOCG—Denominazione di Origine Controllata e Garantita: This is the highest status and guarantees that the wine is of the correct quality and standards.

DOC—Denominazione di Origine Controllata: This is the second-highest status and must meet certain standards and qualities from a specific region.

Vdt—Table Wine: A general category for simple, everyday wine.

New Zealand

Over the last decade, New Zealand has become known for affordable Sauvignon Blancs. It is the most widely planted grape in the Marlborough region and has become a favorite for drinkers of light, fruity wine. Hawke's Bay is one of New Zealand's older and better wine regions and produces some excellent Chardonnay and Cabernets.

Spain

Although known for producing inexpensive wine, many Spanish vineyards have invested in modern winemaking technology to improve quality. Best known is the Tempranillo grape grown in the Rioja region. Garnacha, Graciano and Muzelo can also be found in this region and are often used for blending with Tempranillo. Some Rioja's in this book have the label "Riserva," which means the wine has been aged for more than three years in oak barrels.

California

The most popular American wine region. People spend weeks exploring the central and northern coast. Weather is the key component to producing wines that have little variation from year to year. The most popular areas are the north coast, including Napa and Sonoma; and the central coast, which includes wines from Los Angeles to San Francisco (Monterey, Santa Cruz, San Luis Obispo and Santa Barbara are a few that fall into this category); the Sierra Foothills and Central Valley.

Napa Valley is the best known and produces great Cabernet, Chardonnay, Sauvignon Blanc, Merlot, and Zinfandel. Although there are many spas, resorts, and expensive restaurants, it is still a jewel for the wine world. You can bike around, enjoy picnic lunches, and go from tasting to tasting without spending a lot of money.

Sonoma is Napa's neighbor to the west. The weather is cooler and it produces some excellent Chardonnay

Central California, from Santa Barbara to the Santa Cruz Mountains, is becoming known for its wines, including Chardonnay, Pinot Noir and Zinfandel and Cabernet in Paso Robles.

Oregon

Some of the best Pinot Noir comes from Oregon, especially the Willamette Valley. The Burgundy grape grows well thanks to the cool and cloudy climate, although the area is also known for Pinot Gris, Chardonnay, and Riesling.

Washington

The rain and cool climate are perfect for growing grapes. Columbia Valley is known for its Merlot, Cabernet, Chardonnay, Riesling, and Syrah. Chardonnay and Merlot are also produced in the popular Yakima Valley. Other areas to visit are Walla Walla Valley, Red Mountains, and Columbia Gorge.

Prices

One important skill I have learned from being a *History Detective* and an appraiser is researching comparables. When appraising an object for either historical or replacement value, it is imperative to research similar items in the marketplace. These comparables may be slightly different from the item being appraised, but they can still give you a good idea as to value. All the wines in this book were researched in the same manner. I compared either exact vintages or close years. Although the vintage year can cause price variations in some cases, this was not a significant factor.

I found each wine at multiple stores or on Internet sites with values below $20 (not including shipping or taxes). Even as I was researching and double-checking values for this book, I noticed a fluctuation in prices on a daily basis due to inventory, promotions or other factors.

More then 90% of wines sold in the United States cost less than $15 a bottle.

Elyse's Top 10 Affordable Wine Gifts

1. A bottle under $20.

2. An original, antique corkscrew, can be a whimsical one and you can have fun with this, but remember a simple corkscrew does the job!

3. Contemporary lever-style bottle opener.

4. A decanter.

5. A pair of wine glasses.

6. Wine coasters.

7. Wine charms.

8. An ice bucket to keep your wine cool on a hot summer day!

9. A photo album to place labels of wine in that you drank and loved.

10. A copy of this book!

Thank you ...

There are many, many people who helped me along the way, and to those who I have omitted, please forgive me. However, I would like to give special thanks to a number of people, friends old and new, who made all of this possible.

We have all heard writers mention their editors, some with disdain, others with joy, and I'll join the latter. My editor, Mark Moran, provided fantastic support and assistance and used his magic to create order out of the chaos that I provided him, resulting in a book that I hope you will find informative and enjoyable. He has also become a true friend.

I would also like to thank Zachys and Fritz Hatton for their help in providing me the tools of my trade as a wine auctioneer and introduce me to this world. Zachys also supplied a list of suggestions, all of which I included in this book.

A huge thank you to local wine shops throughout the country for their patience, guidance, and many great suggestions for wines included in this book. Thanks also to all the vineyards, distributors, and marketing departments that assisted me. A special thank you to my local wine shop, Black Tie, in Port Washington, N.Y.

I found that inviting friends and colleagues to wine-tasting parties was a great way to assess wines for this book. In doing my research, I was fortunate to host wine-tasting events in New York, Baltimore, Jupiter, Fla., and Sun Valley, Idaho. Special thanks go to Tim Luke, Greg Strahm, Kenny Marx, Julie and Billy McShane, Dave Rose, Leslie Luray, Steven Luray, Lisa Steinberg, Rachelle Kreiger, and my "Tulane girls" for taking the time to make all of these fun events happen. As a result of some of these wine parties, several individuals made extra efforts to suggest some especially terrific wines included here. Thus, special thanks to Bing Olbum, Richard Bass, Ted Villa, Paige Axelrod, and Halley Bodian.

To Richard, my dear friend, thank you for supplying me the Apple computer that I used to write this book with. I would not have been able to complete this journey without it. To David Binstock, thank you for the endless supply of music that got me through my proofs. There are certain songs that I will not forget and I am now a faithful Pearl Jam fan.

Thanks to photographers Michael Jurick and Shannon Stapleton, who both have an incredible eye behind the camera and gave of their time to shoot pictures for me. I should also mention that they are dear friends of mine.

A big and personal thank you to my friend, Marc Frishman who began and ended this crusade with me. He was the first to download apps, buy wines, spent the entire summer being dragged into wine shops all around the country and then finally took me to Italy to finish this book in Tuscany. I will forever be grateful for those memories.

A special thanks to my good friend and nanny, Carol, for helping with my research while holding down the fort at home and taking care of my boys, Matt and Zach, so that I was able to travel for this book and my History Detective shoots.

Thanks to my parents, Sandy and Allen Luray, not only for their encouragement and many hours of toiling in helping me with planning, research, writing, and tasting to make this effort a success, but thank you the most for just being my parents. I am who I am because of you both and I am the luckiest daughter that you both are my mentors.

To my mother, who taught me how to love, be a mother, and to always see the light in darkness, I thank you and I thank God for you being alive and well. To my father, who has made me the definition, even over 40, of being "daddy's little girl." I cherish our times together in the mountains, our trips with my boys and your constant love and guidance.

At last, but not least, to my sons, Matt and Zach, each my pride and joy in life. There are no words for you both, but as I always say to you when I have to leave for a trip, I hope you always "feel" my love and remember mommy is always in your heart, no matter where she is.

About the Author

Elyse Luray is an appraiser and historian in popular culture. She is one of five hosts on PBS' *History Detectives.* Each week the detectives face new mysteries, intertwining everyday people with the legends of American lore. Mixing forensic evidence with Sherlock Holmes' sharp eye, the History Detectives create entire life stories from a single scrap of evidence, or an overlooked piece of the past, and help people discover the truth about their objects.

Luray is also the appraiser on the yearly HGTV special, *The Longest Yard Sale* and provides appraisals for the HGTV show, *If Walls Could Talk*.

She is a contributor to *The Nate Berkus Show*, helping people appraise objects from their homes. She can also be seen on Rainbow-Media's high-definition satellite service, *VOOM!,* where she hosts, *Treasure Seekers*, attending antique shows around the country. During the hour-long program, she tells viewers what's hot, what to collect and what to pass by.

Luray is a licensed auctioneer and can be seen at the podium selling for many different auction houses including, Bertoia's, Grey Flannel Sports Auctions, and Zachys Wine Auctions. She lends her auctioneering skills to charities throughout the country to help raise money for many different causes, including the Miami Food and Wine Festival and the Chesapeake Bay Wine Classic Foundation.

Before working as a History Detective, she spent 11 years at Christie's auction house as an auctioneer and vice president of the Popular Arts Department. She has also been an appraiser on PBS' *Antiques Roadshow* and the *Early Show* on CBS.

Luray graduated from Tulane University, where she majored in Art History. She is currently on the board of the Deans' Council at Tulane.

Michael Jurick (*www.jurick.net*) photographed Elyse in Wine at 79, 1490 York Ave., New York (*www.wineat79.com*). Jurick is the winner of the Nickelodeon Best Family Photographer Award, and won the "Best of Arts" category at the 2010 Juli B Style Awards.

red
WINES

Sparkling and bright in liquid light

Does the wine our goblets gleam in;

With hue as red as the rosy bed

Which a bee would choose to dream in.

— Charles Fenno Hoffman (1806–1884)

Feudi dei San Gregorio Rubrato Aglianico

This is a soft-textured wine that is a balance of fresh fruit, smoke, and peppers.

We found it for $13.99

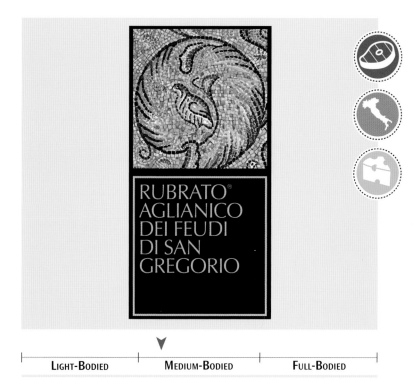

| Light-Bodied | Medium-Bodied | Full-Bodied |

Great with: Grilled meats, lamb, Italian dishes, heavy cheeses, like Brie, Camembert, strong cheddar.

From: Campania, Italy

Made by: Feudi Di San Gregorio

www.feudi.it/en

Pico Maccario
Barbera d'Asti Berro

Strong flavor (cherry), some acidity;
can't beat the price.

We found it for $8.99

| Light-Bodied | Medium-Bodied | Full-Bodied |

Great with: Rich or intense-flavored food. Italian dishes, pizza,
Chinese noodles, meatloaf, roast beef, hamburgers, and Fontina
cheese.

From: Piedmont, Italy

Made by: Pico Maccario

www.picomaccario.com

Cascina 'Tavijn
Barbera d'Asti

Winemaker Nadia Verrua does a great job making this affordable Barbera. It's full of flavor and a great value!

We found it for $17.49

| LIGHT-BODIED | MEDIUM-BODIED | FULL-BODIED |

Great with: Italian dishes, all meats, roasted eggplant, turkey, chili, pork chops, and pizza.

From: Piedmont, Italy

Made by: Cascina 'Tavijn

www.louisdressner.com

Chateau Larose Trintaudon Haut-Médoc (Cru Bourgeois)

This Bordeaux is full of earthy aromas and dark fruit tastes, and a pleasure to drink!

We found it for $11.99

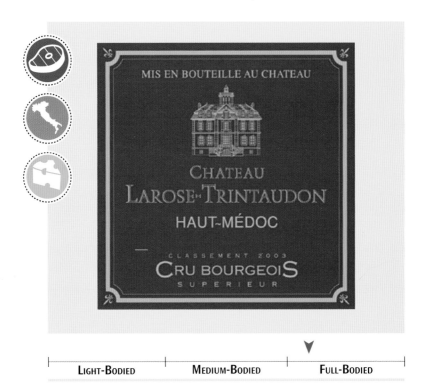

LIGHT-BODIED	MEDIUM-BODIED	FULL-BODIED

Great with: Rich or intense-flavored food. Grilled meats, lamb, pot roast, Italian dishes, hamburgers, meatloaf, and lamb chops.

From: Bordeaux, Haut-Medoc, France

Made by: Chateau Larose Trintaudon

www.chateau-larose-trintaudon.fr

Domaine des Corbillières
Touraine Cabernet Franc

This Cabernet has beautiful aromatics and bold flavors. Delicious to drink while young and fresh. A perfect French Cabernet!

We found it for $12.99

Light-Bodied	Medium-Bodied	Full-Bodied

Great with: Rich or intense-flavored food. Roasted chicken, skirt steak, pork chops, or foie gras, or after dinner with crème brûlée.

From: Loire Valley, France

Made by: Domaine des Corbillières

www.robertkacherselections.com

J. Lohr Seven Oaks
Cabernet Sauvignon

A favorite of many, it has the taste of black cherry, other fruit
flavors, and a bit of vanilla. It gets better as it breathes.

We found it for $7.10

| LIGHT-BODIED | MEDIUM-BODIED | FULL-BODIED |

Great with: Rich or intense-flavored food. Grilled meats, lamb, pot
roast, Italian dishes, London broil, and tomato-basil chicken.

From: San Jose, Calif.

Made by: J. Lohr Vineyards & Wines

www.jlohr.com

Finnegan's Lake Cabernet Sauvignon

A fruity, smooth, ripe, and rich wine.
A great wine for the money.

We found it for $12.99

LIGHT-BODIED	MEDIUM-BODIED	FULL-BODIED

Great with: Rich or intense-flavored food. Grilled meats, lamb,
pot roast, Italian dishes, chicken in garlic sauce, sweet-and-sour
chicken, and heavy cheeses, like Brie, gouda, and strong cheddar.

From: California

Made by: Finnegan's Lake

www.sherbrookecellars.com

Seventy-Five Wine Co. Cabernet Sauvignon

This wine has great, full flavor with a taste of fruit; rich, a great wine for an evening of pleasure.

We found it for $16.99

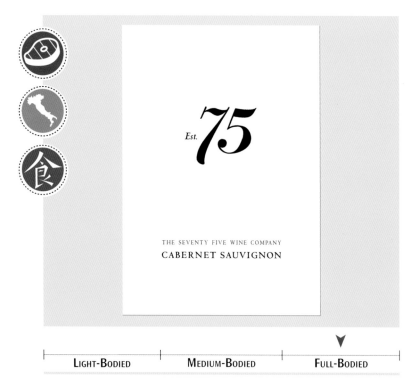

THE SEVENTY FIVE WINE COMPANY
CABERNET SAUVIGNON

| LIGHT-BODIED | MEDIUM-BODIED | FULL-BODIED |

Great with: Rich or intense-flavored food. Grilled meats, lamb, game, Italian dishes, sweet-and-sour pork and heavy cheeses, like Brie, gouda, and gorgonzola.

From: St. Helena, Calif.

Made by: Tuck Beckstoffer Wines

www.75wine.com

Kangarilla Road
Cabernet Sauvignon

A full-bodied wine with fruit,
spice, and lots of flavor!

We found it for $14.99

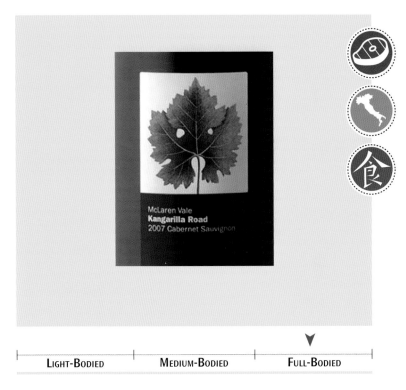

| LIGHT-BODIED | MEDIUM-BODIED | FULL-BODIED |

Great with: Rich or intense-flavored food. Filet mignon, lamb, chops,
Italian dishes, Moo Shu pork, and dark chocolate.

From: McLaren Vale, Australia

Made by: Kangarilla Road

www.kangarillaroad.com.au

Bogle
Cabernet Sauvignon

This wine needs to breathe and gets better with time; rich and spicy, perfect flavors.

We found it for $8.04

A Top 10 Red

LIGHT-BODIED	MEDIUM-BODIED	FULL-BODIED

Great with: Rich or intense-flavored food. Smoked meats, lamb, chops, Italian dishes, hamburgers, pasta, heavy cheeses, and gumbo.

From: Clarksburg, Calif.

Made by: Bogle

www.boglewinery.com

Ex-Libris
Cabernet Sauvignon

A bold Cabernet, nice balance,
with intense fruit.

We found it for $13.25

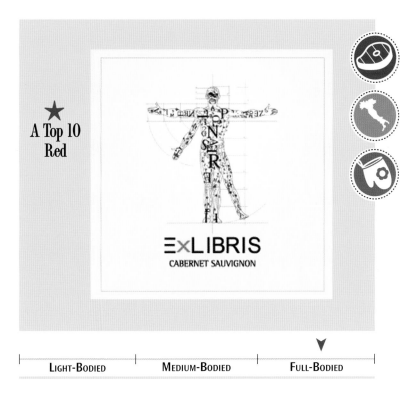

★
**A Top 10
Red**

⊟×LIBRIS
CABERNET SAUVIGNON

LIGHT-BODIED	MEDIUM-BODIED	FULL-BODIED ▼

Great with: Rich or intense-flavored food. Grilled meats, lamb, pot
    roast, Italian dishes, Chinese-style meats and heavy cheeses, Brie,
    gouda, and parmesan.

From: Columbia Valley, Wash.

Made by: Ex-Libris

Kendall-Jackson Vintner's Reserve Cabernet Sauvignon

Deep assorted cherry flavors; intense, bold, the perfect Cabernet for the price!

We found it for $12.94

| LIGHT-BODIED | MEDIUM-BODIED | FULL-BODIED |

Great with: Rich or intense-flavored food. Grilled meats, lamb, pot roast, Italian dishes, Chinese-style meats and heavy cheeses, like Brie, Camembert, and strong cheddar.

From: Sonoma County, Calif.

Made by: Kendall-Jackson

www.kj.com

Folie a' Deux
Cabernet Sauvignon

This wine has good balance with a taste of black cherry and a wonderful lingering taste.

We found it for $11.99

| LIGHT-BODIED | MEDIUM-BODIED | FULL-BODIED |

Great with: Rich or intense-flavored food. Grilled meats, roasted pork, beef stew, tomato sauces, venison, gorgonzola cheese, and walnuts.

From: Napa Valley, Calif.

Made by: Folie a' Deux

www.folieadeux.com

Napa Cellars
Cabernet Sauvignon

A wine with wonderful fruit flavors of blackberries and plums, with hints of bittersweet chocolate.

We found it for $5.10

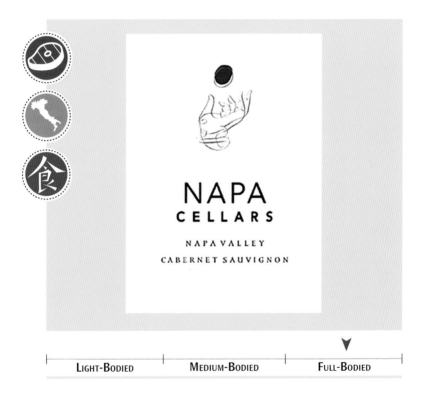

LIGHT-BODIED	MEDIUM-BODIED	FULL-BODIED

Great with: Rich or intense-flavored food. Grilled meats, lamb, chops, Italian dishes, Chinese-style meats including Szechuan chicken.

From: Napa Valley, Calif.

Made by: Napa Cellars

www.napacellars.com

Wyatt
Cabernet Sauvignon

What a find! This wine is smoky, spicy with some fruit flavors, and right for the price!

We found it for $9.98

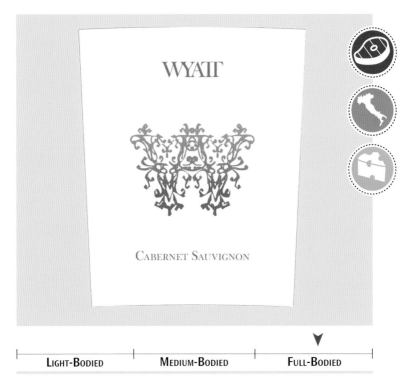

| LIGHT-BODIED | MEDIUM-BODIED | FULL-BODIED |

Great with: Rich or intense-flavored food. Lamb, roasted eggplant, Italian dishes, hamburgers, Chinese-style dishes and cheeses, like Brie, strong cheddar, and gorgonzola, or chicken in brown sauce.

From: Oakville, Calif.

Made by: Wyatt

www.polanerselections.com

Joel Gott
Cabernet Sauvignon

This wine is balanced with a velvety finish.
It is rich and ripe with some flavors of fruit.

We found it for $13.95

|LIGHT-BODIED|MEDIUM-BODIED|FULL-BODIED|

Great with: Rich or intense-flavored food. Grilled meats, lamb, pot roast, Italian dishes, hamburgers, chili, Moo Shu pork, and veggie burgers.

From: Napa Valley, Calif.

Made by: Joel Gott

www.gottwines.com

Main Street Winery Cabernet Sauvignon

This wine is well balanced, rich, and ripe with flavors of black cherry and plum.

We found it for $9.99

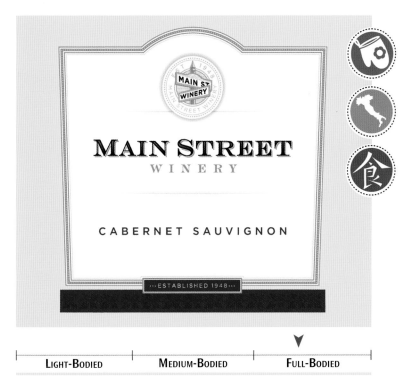

LIGHT-BODIED	MEDIUM-BODIED	FULL-BODIED

Great with: Rich or intense-flavored food. Meats like venison and rib eye, broccoli, Italian dishes, beef stew, cheddar, Brie, and gorgonzola cheese.

From: St. Helena, Calif.

Made by: Main Street Winery

www.mainstwinery.com

Pedroncelli
Cabernet Sauvignon

Aromas of ripe plum, black currant, and toasty oak;
concentrated flavors, simply elegant.

We found it for $9.49

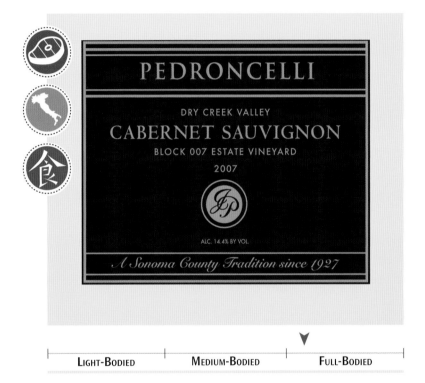

| LIGHT-BODIED | MEDIUM-BODIED | FULL-BODIED |

Great with: Rich or intense-flavored food. Grilled meats, lamb, pot
roast, Italian dishes, Chinese-style meats, and heavy cheeses, like
Brie, Camembert, and strong cheddar.

From: Geyserville, Calif.

Made by: Pedroncelli Winery & Vineyards

www.pedroncelli.com

Primus
Cabernet Blend

This wine is rich with ripe fruit flavors, and
exotic spices—love the blend of the grapes. A favorite!

We found it for $9.39

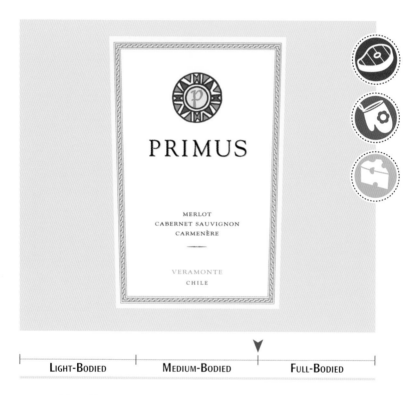

| LIGHT-BODIED | MEDIUM-BODIED | FULL-BODIED |

Great with: Grilled meats, lamb, chicken, game, pastas, hamburgers,
pot roast, and turkey meatloaf.

From: Colchagua Valley, Chile

Made by: Veramonte

www.veramonte.com

Columbia Crest Grand Estates Cabernet Sauvignon

Nice spices, well balanced
with a long, lingering taste.

We found it for $9.99

| LIGHT-BODIED | MEDIUM-BODIED | FULL-BODIED |

Great with: Grilled meats, lamb, pot roast, Italian dishes, barbecue,
roast beef, and chicken.

From: Paterson, Wash.

Made by: Columbia Crest

www.columbiacrest.com

Cantine Colosi
Sicilia Rosso

Wine that is full of flavor with a sweet cherry taste.
Terrific quality for the money!

We found it for $12.99

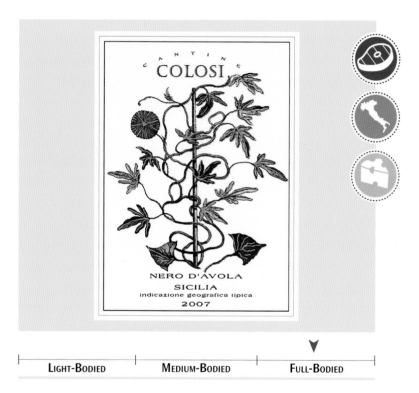

Light-Bodied	Medium-Bodied	Full-Bodied

Great with: Red meats cooked any style, pasta with tomato sauce
and aged cheese. Italian dishes, chicken parmesan, pizza, and
meatloaf.

From: Sicily, Italy

Made by: Cantine Colosi

www.cantinecolosi.com

Cantine Colosi
Cariddi Rosso

A great Italian wine with the perfect balance
of fruit and spice.

We found it for $9.99

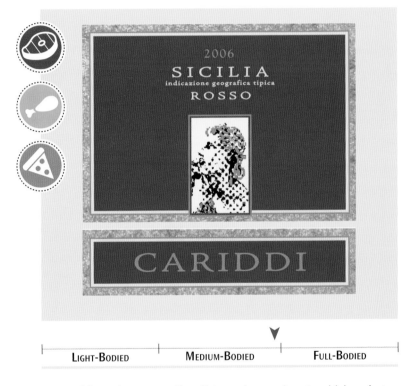

| LIGHT-BODIED | MEDIUM-BODIED | FULL-BODIED |

Great with: Red meats, Italian dishes, pizza and pasta, chicken, hot
  dogs, and hamburgers.

From: Sicily, Italy

Made by: Cantine Colosi

www.cantinecolosi.com

Latium Morini Valpolicella Superiore Campo Prognai

Valpolicella is wonderful, filled with ripe, dark fruit, and oak tastes; well balanced and a great find at this price!

We found it for $15

	V	
LIGHT-BODIED	MEDIUM-BODIED	FULL-BODIED

Great with: Pasta and other Italian dishes, pizza, chicken, eggplant, all red meats, beef in garlic sauce, and cashew chicken.

From: Veneto, Italy

Made by: Latium

Condesa de Leganza Crianza

A red Spanish wine with cinnamon touches.
The flavor evolves as it breathes.

We found it for $9.49

| LIGHT-BODIED | MEDIUM-BODIED | FULL-BODIED |

Great with: Casual food, including pizza, pasta, sausage, fajitas,
burritos, and barbeque. Also pairs well with grilled seafood.

From: Toledo, Spain

Made by: Condesa De Leganza

www.bodegasleganza.com

Roagna
Dolcetto D'Alba

Fruity yet not too sweet. It is well balanced
and a perfect wine to drink all the time!

We found it for $15

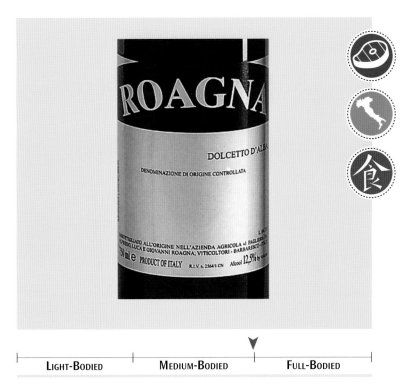

| LIGHT-BODIED | MEDIUM-BODIED | FULL-BODIED |

Great with: Italian dishes, grilled meats and chicken, appetizers,
pizza, eggplant, and parmesan cheese.

From: Piedmont, Italy

Made by: Roagna

www.roagna.com

Louis Jadot Moulin-à-Vent
Chateau des Jacques

This wine is 100% Gamay grapes, making it fruity, well balanced, with good aroma.

We found it for $19.95

| LIGHT-BODIED | MEDIUM-BODIED | FULL-BODIED |

Great with: Rich or intense-flavored food. Grilled meats, lamb, pot roast, Italian dishes, Chinese-style meats, and heavy cheeses, like Brie, gorgonzola, and strong cheddar.

From: Beaujolais, France

Made by: Louis Jadot

www.louisjadot.com

Domaine Grand Veneur
Les Champauvins

What a find! This ripe red blend is smooth with a licorice and spice flavor. A true bargain for this type!

We found it for $14.95

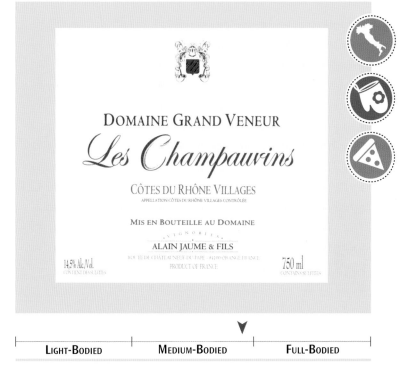

| LIGHT-BODIED | MEDIUM-BODIED | FULL-BODIED |

Great with: All types of meat, Italian dishes, grilled seafood with heavy sauces, and mild to medium cheeses.

From: Côtes du Rhône, France

Made by: Domaine Grand Veneur

www.domaine-grand-veneur.com

Chateau Cambis
Côtes du Rhône Villages

Yet another wonderful find, this blend has lots of body. It is spicy, silky, and has great flavor!

We found it for $11.19

| LIGHT-BODIED | MEDIUM-BODIED | FULL-BODIED |

Great with: Intense-flavored foods including grilled meats, lamb, pot roast, Italian dishes, Chinese-style meats, and heavy cheeses such as Brie, Camembert, and strong cheddar.

From: Côtes du Rhône, France

Made by: Chateau Cambis

www.zachys.com

E. Guigal
Côtes du Rhône Rosé

A well-rounded dry blend with elegance, strength, and balance, plus a great spicy flavor.

We found it for $9.17

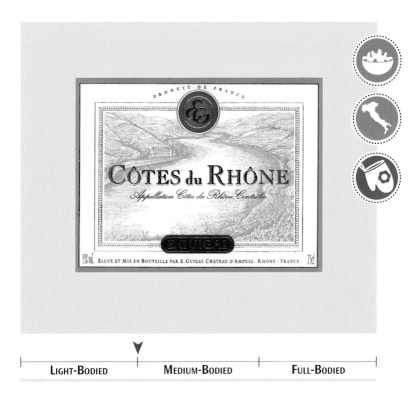

| LIGHT-BODIED | MEDIUM-BODIED | FULL-BODIED |

Great with: Salads, light pastas, and grilled kabobs.

From: Côtes du Rhône, France

Made by: E. Guigal

www.guigal.com

Las Rocas de San Alejandro Garnacha (Grenache)

A medium- to full-bodied wine filled with flavor, including raspberries, and peppers.

We found it for $8.44

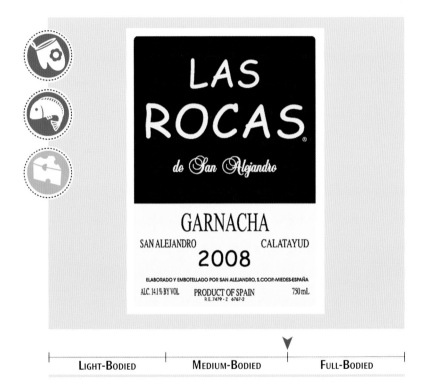

LIGHT-BODIED   MEDIUM-BODIED   FULL-BODIED

Great with: Grilled meats and chicken, stews, pot roast, meatloaf, and hamburgers.

From: Beaujolais, France

Made by: Las Rocas

www.san-alejandro.com

Sella and Mosca Cannonau di Sardegna Riserva (Grenache)

This wine is well balanced
and rich with ripe, plum flavors.

We found it for $10.74

| LIGHT-BODIED | MEDIUM-BODIED | FULL-BODIED |

Great with: Casual food, including pizza, pasta, sausage, fajitas,
burritos and barbeque. Also pairs well with grilled seafood and
Italian dishes.

From: Sardinia, Italy

Made by: Sella and Mosca

www.sellaandmosca.com

The Derelict Vineyard Grenache

Rich flavor, with fruit and spice, overall softness and better with time.

We found it for $19.98

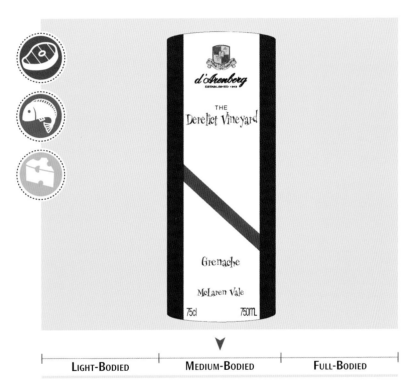

| LIGHT-BODIED | MEDIUM-BODIED | FULL-BODIED |

Great with: Barbecued meat, pasta, grilled seafood, bacon, mild cheeses, and pork chops.

From: McLaren Vale, South Australia

Made by: d'Arenberg

www.darenberg.com.au

Domaine D'Andezon
Côtes du Rhône

This wine is rich, spicy and delightful,
a mix of Grenache and Syrah.

We found it for $10.32

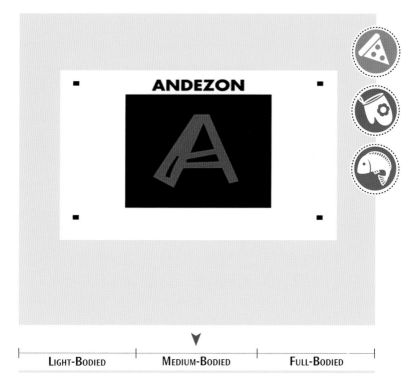

LIGHT-BODIED	MEDIUM-BODIED	FULL-BODIED

Great with: Casual food, including pizza, pasta, sausage, fajitas,
burritos and barbeque. Also pairs well with grilled seafood and
hamburgers.

From: Côtes du Rhône, France

Made by: Domaine D'Andezon

www.polanerselections.com

D'Andezon Côtes du Rhône Villages La Granacha Signargues (Grenache)

This well-balanced wine is peppery, sexy, and sensational. A great bargain and superb!

We found it for $12.99

LIGHT-BODIED · MEDIUM-BODIED · FULL-BODIED

Great with: Italian dishes, barbecue, chicken or ribs, pizza, all meats including ham, and grilled lobster.

From: Côtes du Rhône, France

Made by: Domaine D'Andezon

www.polanerselections.com

Domaine de la Petite Cassagne Rouge

This spicy wine—Grenache (30%), Syrah (30%), Carignan (40%)—has a raspberry and licorice taste, is rich and has a good finish—delicious!

We found it for $9.98

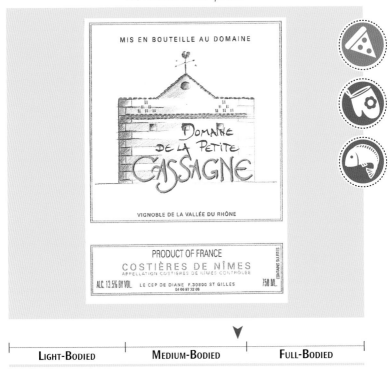

Light-Bodied	Medium-Bodied	Full-Bodied

Great with: Casual food, including pizza, pasta, sausage, fajitas, burritos, and barbeque. Also pairs well with grilled seafood.

From: Costières de Nîmes, France

Made by: Domaine de la Petite Cassagne

www.robertkacherselections.com

Bodega Catena Zapata Malbec

This is a smooth wine with good spices that compliment but do not overpower. Very drinkable!

We found it for $14.99

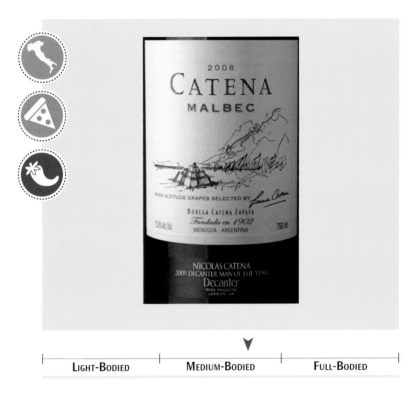

| LIGHT-BODIED | MEDIUM-BODIED | FULL-BODIED |

Great with: Italian dishes, pizza, steak, Mexican food, and Indian flavored dishes.

From: Mendoza, Argentina

Made by: Catena Zapata

www.catenawines.com

Crios de Susana Balbo Malbec

Fruity, elegant, and spicy. Simply perfect for every occasion.

We found it for $13.99

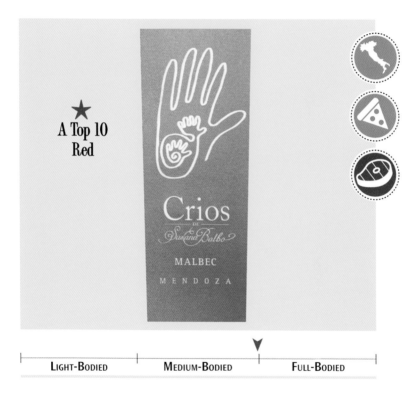

★
A Top 10 Red

LIGHT-BODIED | MEDIUM-BODIED | FULL-BODIED

Great with: Italian dishes, pizza, steak, all grilled meats, Mediterranean foods and sauces, and (similar to Cabernet) pairs well with intense flavors.

From: Agrelo, Mendoza, Argentina

Made by: Crios

www.dominiodelplata.com

La Posta
Malbec

This wine has a great lingering flavor, with tastes of cinnamon, pepper, and black cherry. A favorite Malbec!

We found it for $17.28

★
A Top 10
Red

LIGHT-BODIED	MEDIUM-BODIED	▼ FULL-BODIED

Great with: Hamburgers and chicken to pizza and mild cheeses, pairs well with Italian dishes, pizza, steak, all grilled meats, Mediterranean foods and sauces, and with intense flavors.

From: Mendoza, Argentina

Made by: Pizzaella Family Vineyard

www.lapostavineyards.com

Felino Viña Cobos Malbec

This wine is full of flavor: fruity with a mix of raspberries and hints of ginger pepper.

We found it for $15.95

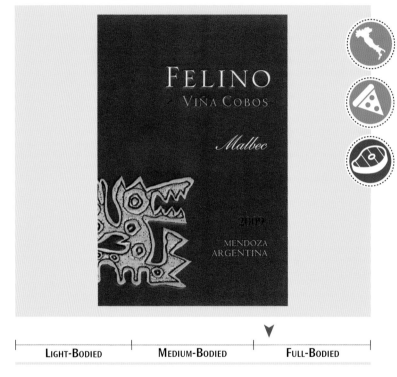

| LIGHT-BODIED | MEDIUM-BODIED | FULL-BODIED |

Great with: Intense flavors, Italian dishes, pizza, steak, all grilled meats, hamburgers, nachos, Cajun, and jambalaya.

From: Mendoza, Argentina

Made by: Viña Cobos

www.vinacobos.com

Pulenta Estate La Flor Malbec

This wine shows some spices and is fruity, with currant and black cherry.

We found it for $9.99

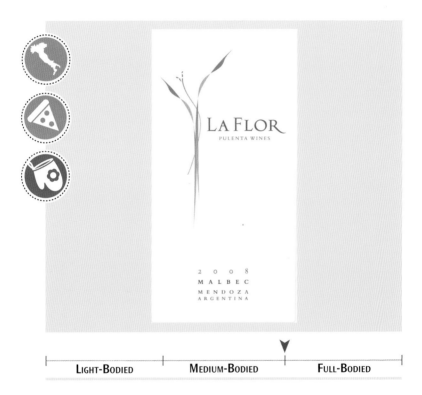

| | MEDIUM-BODIED | ▼ |
| LIGHT-BODIED | MEDIUM-BODIED | FULL-BODIED |

Great with: Italian dishes, pizza, steak, all grilled meats, Mexican and Indian dishes, tacos, and hamburgers.

From: Mendoza, Argentina

Made by: Pulenta Estate

www.pulentaestate.com

Tikal
Patriota

A blended wine—Bonarda (60%), Malbec (40%)—dense and rich, full of flavor with some raspberry and chocolate.

We found it for $15.97

	LIGHT-BODIED	MEDIUM-BODIED	FULL-BODIED

Great with: Beef fajitas, barbecued chicken, Italian dishes, pizza, steak, all grilled meats, smoked ham, and pork chops.

From: Mendoza, Argentina

Made by: Tikal

www.tikalwines.com

Kendall-Jackson Vintner's Reserve Meritage

Tastes of vanilla with hints of blackberry, black licorice, plum and cherry. Some say it tastes like Bordeaux!

We found it for $10.99

| LIGHT-BODIED | MEDIUM-BODIED | FULL-BODIED |

Great with: Intense-flavored food, grilled meats, lamb, pot roast, Italian dishes, Chinese-style meats, and dark chocolates.

From: Sonoma County, Calif.

Made by: Kendall-Jackson

www.kj.com

Frei Brothers Reserve
Dry Creek Valley Merlot

This wine has blackberry touches and fruit flavors that evolve as it breathes. A wine you will enjoy as the meal continues.

We found it for $12.99

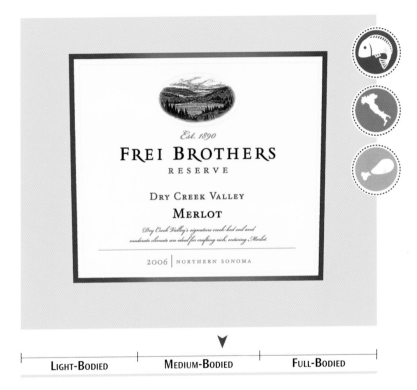

| LIGHT-BODIED | MEDIUM-BODIED | FULL-BODIED |

Great with: Mild to rich-flavored foods. It goes well with grilled salmon, but can also be paired with turkey, lamb chops, and Italian dishes. Some like it with Chinese as well.

From: Sonoma, Calif.

Made by: Frei Brothers

www.freibrothers.com

Wild Horse
Merlot

A nice wine with rich, ripe fruit flavors. Well balanced. A great value for the price!

We found it for $7.23

Light-Bodied	Medium-Bodied	Full-Bodied

Great with: Grilled swordfish steak, lamb chops, Swiss, Romano, Gruyere cheese, or chicken in garlic sauce.

From: Paso Robles, Calif.

Made by: Wild Horse Winery

www.wildhorsewinery.com

Montes Alpha
Merlot

Nice flavor with a touch of vanilla, followed by a long and smooth finish. Very, very elegant.

We found it for $9.97

| Light-Bodied | Medium-Bodied | Full-Bodied |

Great with: Jalapenos, steak, pork, pizza, and potato skins.

From: Santa Cruz, Chile

Made by: Apalta Winery and Vineyards Viña Montes

www.monteswines.com

Blackstone Winery
Sonoma Reserve Merlot

This wine is velvety with a black cherry flavor,
smoky yet smooth.

We found it for $4.99

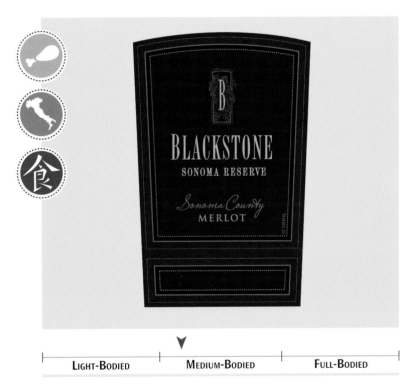

| LIGHT-BODIED | MEDIUM-BODIED | FULL-BODIED |

Great with: Mild to rich-flavored foods. It goes well with grilled
salmon, rack of lamb, quesadillas, pork chops, Swiss and Monterey
Jack cheese, and Italian dishes. Some like it with Chinese as well.

From: Napa Valley, Calif.

Made by: Blackstone Winery

www.blackstonewinery.com

Kendall-Jackson
Vintner's Reserve Merlot

This wine is smooth with refined flavors of cherry, chocolate and plums—great wine for the price!

We found it for $8.99

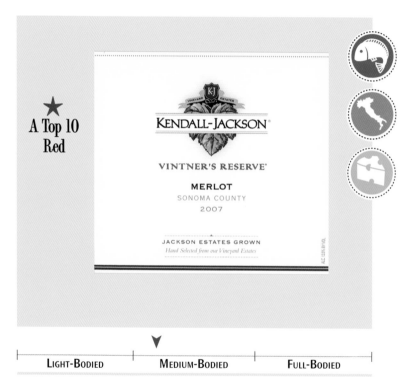

★
A Top 10 Red

Light-Bodied	Medium-Bodied	Full-Bodied

Great with: Mild to rich-flavored foods. It goes well with grilled swordfish, but can also be paired with turkey, lamb chops, and Italian dishes. Goes well with most cheeses.

From: Sonoma County, Calif.

Made by: Kendall-Jackson

www.kj.com

Rodney Strong
Merlot

This wine is ripe and rich with flavors of plum and blueberries, plus hints of spicy vanilla—an excellent Merlot!

We found it for $12.79

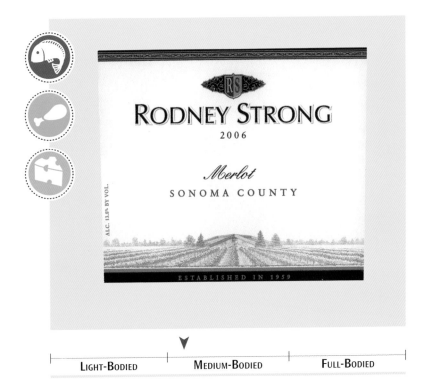

| LIGHT-BODIED | MEDIUM-BODIED | FULL-BODIED |

Great with: Mild to rich-flavored foods. It goes well with grilled salmon, but can also be paired with pork chops, lamb chops, steak, pizza, pasta, Swiss, Romano or Gruyere cheese, chicken.

From: Sonoma, Calif.

Made by: Rodney Strong

www.rodneystrong.com

Casa Lapostolle
Cuvée Alexandre Merlot

This Merlot has favors of dark cherry, plum,
smoky minerals and is nicely balanced.

We found it for $16.98

| LIGHT-BODIED | MEDIUM-BODIED | FULL-BODIED |

Great with: Mild to rich-flavored foods. It goes well with grilled tuna,
Italian dishes, flavored stews, chicken dishes with sauces, and
hamburgers.

From: Santa Cruz, Chile

Made by: Casa Lapostolle

www.casalapostolle.com

Newton
Napa Valley Claret

A Merlot blend, light, refined, and balanced with a taste of
black and red currants, licorice, and blueberry.

We found it for $14.98

| LIGHT-BODIED | MEDIUM-BODIED | FULL-BODIED |

Great with: Mild to rich-flavored foods. It goes well with grilled
salmon, but can also be paired with turkey, quesadillas, pork chops,
Swiss and Monterey Jack cheese, lamb chops, and Italian dishes.

From: Napa Valley, Calif.

Made by: Newton Vineyard

www.newtonvineyard.com

Fosso Corno Mayro Montepulciano d'Abruzzo

Well balanced with tastes of blackberries, cherries, and wood. Perfect starter Italian wine.

We found it for $11.99

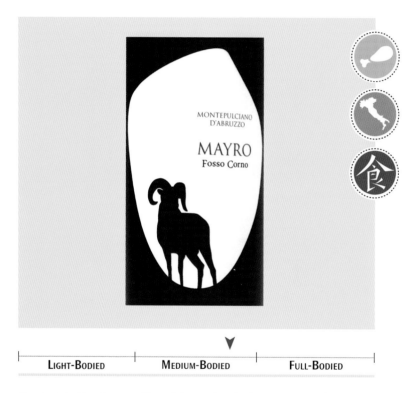

| LIGHT-BODIED | MEDIUM-BODIED | FULL-BODIED |

Great with: Eggplant, Italian dishes, salami, pizza, mozzarella cheese, veal, chicken Marsala, and steak.

From: Montepulciano, Italy

Made by: Fosso Corno

www.giulianaimports.com

Erath
Pinot Noir

A perfect Oregon Pinot. Zesty spice, fruit, and smoky flavors.

We found it for $14.94

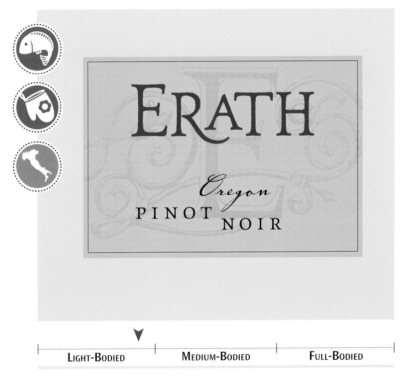

| LIGHT-BODIED | MEDIUM-BODIED | FULL-BODIED |

Great with: Grilled seafood, smoky dishes like barbeque, bacon, ribs, light pastas, and baked ham.

From: Willamette Valley, Ore.

Made by: Erath Winery

www.erath.com

Wyatt
Pinot Noir

Earthy with some fruit taste, yet very refreshing!

We found it for $13.25

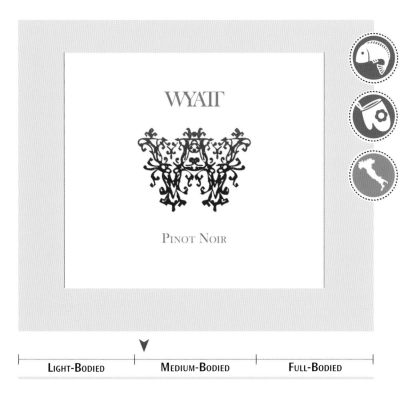

| LIGHT-BODIED | MEDIUM-BODIED | FULL-BODIED |

Great with: Grilled seafood, rosemary chicken, barbeque, light pastas, and cheese.

From: Oakville, Calif.

Made by: Wyatt

Bourgogne Pinot Noir

Excellent Pinot for the price: light, flows well, silky with a nice even balance.

We found it for $9.99

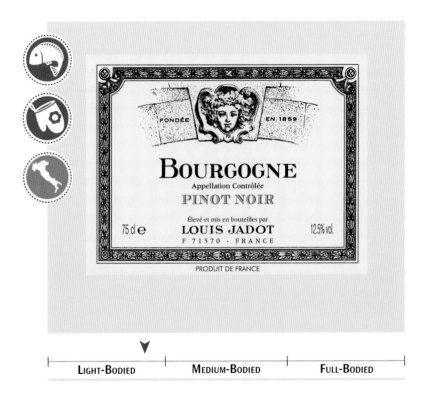

| LIGHT-BODIED | MEDIUM-BODIED | FULL-BODIED |

Great with: Light pasta, poached or grilled salmon, bacon, ribs, baked ham, and grilled chicken.

From: Burgundy, France

Made by: Louis Jadot

www.louisjadot.com

Napa Cellars
Pinot Noir

Delicate, some fruit flavor, strawberry,
cherry, and sweet spice at the finish.

We found it for $5.39

LIGHT-BODIED | MEDIUM-BODIED | FULL-BODIED

Great with: Pan-seared duck breast or simply prepared salmon
   dishes, and grilled chicken.

From: Napa Valley, Calif.

Made by: Napa Cellars

www.napacellars.com

MacMurray Ranch
Pinot Noir

A nice Pinot with black pepper taste.
A pleasing, easy-to-drink earthy wine.

We found it for $12.42

LIGHT-BODIED | MEDIUM-BODIED | FULL-BODIED

Great with: Rack of lamb, grilled salmon, and Shitake mushroom risotto, nice with simple appetizers.

From: Russian River, Calif.

Made by: MacMurray Ranch

www.macmurrayranch.com

Estancia
Pinot Noir

This wine is excellent, delightful, and unobtrusive. It has some cherry flavor.

We found it for $11.99

★
A Top 10
Red

2009
PINOT NOIR
MONTEREY COUNTY
PINNACLES RANCHES
HANDCRAFTED ARTISAN GROWN

LIGHT-BODIED	MEDIUM-BODIED	FULL-BODIED

Great with: Grilled seafood, smoky dishes like barbeque, bacon, ribs, light pastas, and baked ham.

From: Paso Robles, Calif.

Made by: Estancia

www.estancialajolla.com

Cloudline
Pinot Noir

A great everyday wine, light but feels full-bodied, with fruity, well-balanced flavors.

We found it for $13.99

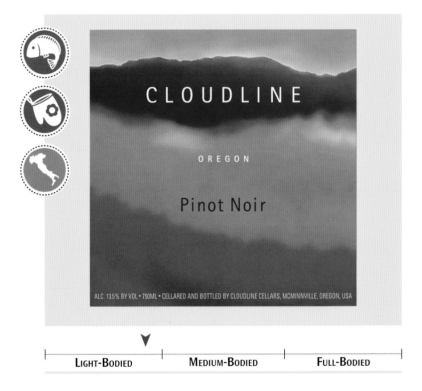

| LIGHT-BODIED | MEDIUM-BODIED | FULL-BODIED |

Great with: Grilled chicken, poached salmon, barbeque, bacon, ribs, light pastas, and baked ham.

From: Willamette Valley, Ore.

Made by: Cloudline Cellars

www.dreyfusashby.com

Innocent Bystander
Pinot Noir

A favorite of many. It has a delicious cherry taste and juicy, young flavor that lasts!

We found it for $14.79

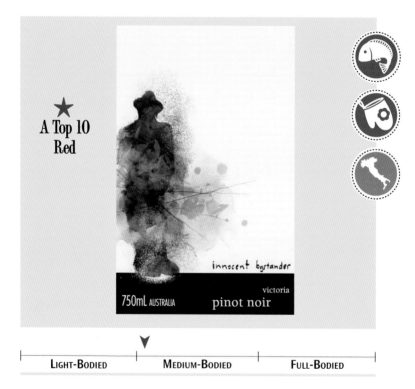

★
A Top 10
Red

Great with: Grilled seafood, rosemary chicken, light pastas, and Peking duck.

From: Yarra Valley, Australia

Made by: Innocent Bystander Winemakers

www.innocentbystander.com.au

Montes Alpha
Pinot Noir

Intense aroma with tastes of raspberry and black cherry.
Well balanced and very impressive!

We found it for $14.21

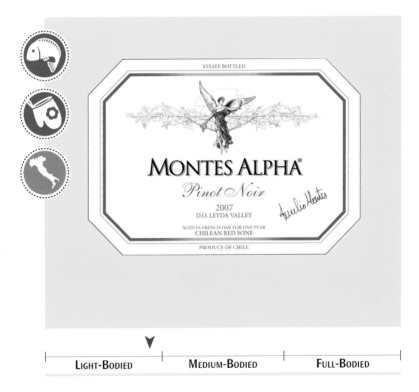

| LIGHT-BODIED | MEDIUM-BODIED | FULL-BODIED |

Great with: Grilled seafood, barbeque, ribs, light pastas, baked ham,
mac and cheese, and pizza.

From: Santa Cruz, Chile

Made by: Apalta Winery and Vineyards Viña Montes

www.monteswines.com

d'Autrefois
Pinot Noir

Rich, deep, powerful fruit flavor, earthy and spicy! Full of black cherry. A great French "country wine."

We found it for $12.50

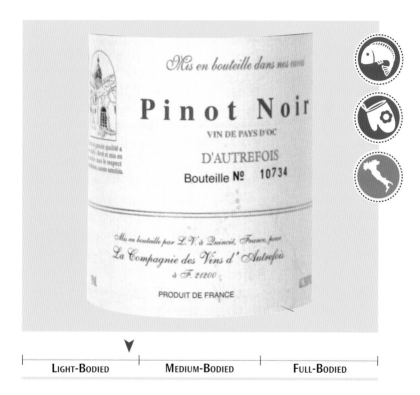

LIGHT-BODIED	MEDIUM-BODIED	FULL-BODIED

Great with: Grilled seafood, grilled pork loin, light pastas, and turkey.

From: Burgundy, France

Made by: Vins d'Autrefois

www.champagne-laherte.com

Faustino V
Reserva Rioja

A wine that is velvety, meaty,
robust yet smooth.

We found it for $11.99

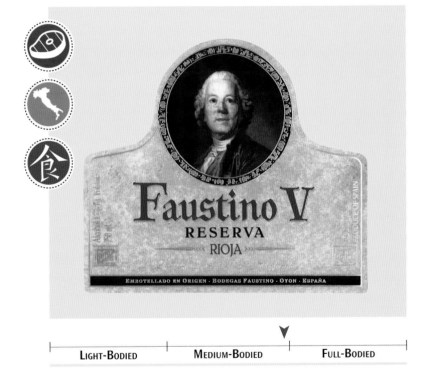

| LIGHT-BODIED | MEDIUM-BODIED | FULL-BODIED |

Great with: Grilled meats, casseroles, Italian dishes, Moo Shu pork,
and paella.

From: Rioja, Spain

Made by: Faustino

www.bodegasfaustino.com

Bodegas Muga
Rioja Rosado

A great, refreshing Rosé with fruit flavors.
A perfect wine for a summer day!

We found it for $18.99

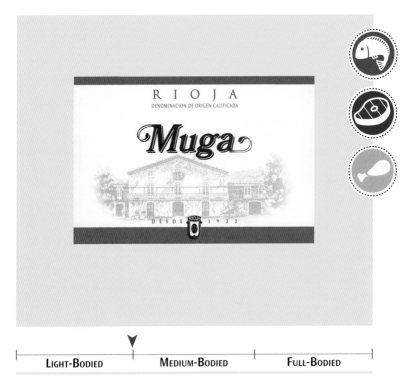

| LIGHT-BODIED | MEDIUM-BODIED | FULL-BODIED |

Great with: Grilled salmon, roast beef, lamb, duck and mushrooms, salads, seafood, and paella.

From: Rioja, Spain

Made by: Muga Winery

www.bodegasmuga.com

Castello di Bossi
Chianti Classico

This Sangiovese needs to breathe, but becomes a wonderful strong flavor; rich flavors of fruit, spices, and tobacco.

We found it for $10.74

| LIGHT-BODIED | MEDIUM-BODIED | FULL-BODIED |

Great with: Italian dishes, hamburgers, pizza, parmesan, mozzarella, and fontina cheese.

From: Tuscany, Italy

Made by: Castello di Bossi Spa

www.castellodibossi.it

Rosso di Montalcino
Col d' Orcia Cinzano

A nice, red Sangiovese wine with ripe fruit taste and sweetness.
One of Tuscany's favorite wines at restaurants.

We found it for $15.99

| LIGHT-BODIED | MEDIUM-BODIED | FULL-BODIED |

Great with: Grilled meats, lamb, pot roast, Italian dishes, Chinese-style meats, pizza, eggplant, and lasagna.

From: Tuscany, Italy

Made by: Col d' Orcia

www.coldorcia.it

Ricasoli Brolio
Chianti Classico

This Tuscan Sangiovese wine has plenty of fruit and tannins,
and a very pleasant finish that lingers on your palate.

We found it for $16.95

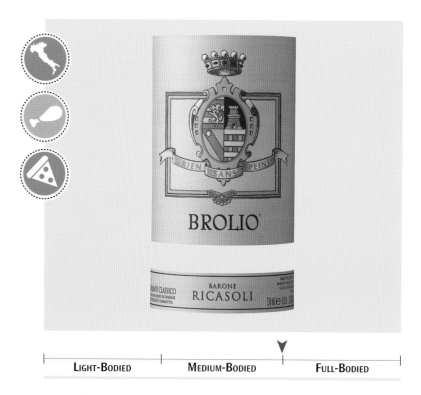

| LIGHT-BODIED | MEDIUM-BODIED | FULL-BODIED |

Great with: Pasta and other Italian dishes, lasagna, pizza,
   hamburgers, fontina, mozzarella, and provolone cheese.

From: Tuscany, Italy

Made by: Barone Ricasoli

www.ricasoli.it

Monte Antico
Rosso

A blend of Sangiovese, Merlot and Cabernet Sauvignon, with berry and cherry flavors. Spicy, elegant, and fruity.

We found it for $7.91

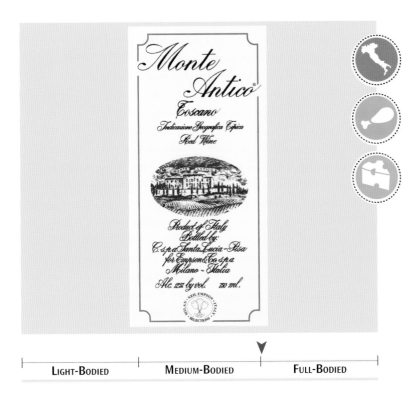

| LIGHT-BODIED | MEDIUM-BODIED | FULL-BODIED |

Great with: Pasta or risotto, chicken, meat and cheese, Italian dishes, pizza, and hamburgers.

From: Tuscany, Italy

Made by: Monte Antico

www.monteanticowine.com

Nipozzano Riserva
Chianti Rufina

A rich Sangiovese wine with taste of fruit flavors, including
black cherry, plum and raspberry—spicy and crisp.

We found it for $17.04

| LIGHT-BODIED | MEDIUM-BODIED | FULL-BODIED |

Great with: Barbecued meats, stews and cheeses, and Italian dishes.

From: Firenze, Italy

Made by: Marchesi de' Frescobaldi

www.frescobaldi.it

Ruffino Riserva Ducale Chianti Classico

This well-known Sangiovese wine is balanced and velvety with a fruity core. Bold and delicious!

We found it for $11.88

| Light-Bodied | Medium-Bodied | Full-Bodied |

Great with: Pasta and other Italian dishes, pizza, eggplant, hamburgers, mozzarella, provolone, and fontina cheese.

From: Tuscany, Italy
Made by: Ruffino

www.ruffino.it

Great Wines Under $20 • 101

Poggio Stella Vino Nobile di Montepulciano

This Sangiovese wine has rich cherry or plum-like flavors and aromas.

We found it for $19.99

| LIGHT-BODIED | MEDIUM-BODIED | FULL-BODIED |

Great with: Pasta and other Italian dishes, mozzarella, and provolone cheese.

From: Tuscany, Italy

Made by: Poggio Stella

www.palmbayimport.com

Bere
Tuscan Red Viticcio

This blend of Sangiovese and Cabernet has character. Great for causal drinking. Strong but smooth. Perfect Italian wine!

We found it for $11.95

| LIGHT-BODIED | MEDIUM-BODIED | FULL-BODIED |

Great with: Intensely flavored foods, including Italian dishes, barbeque, grilled seafood and meats, pizza, burgers, and pastas.

From: Firenze, Italy

Made by: Fattoria Viticcio S.r.l.

www.fattoriaviticcio.com

Poliziano
Rosso di Montepulciano

This blend of Sangiovese and Merlot is fresh, balanced, and fruity—a delight full of flavor!

We found it for $11.99

| LIGHT-BODIED | MEDIUM-BODIED | FULL-BODIED |

Great with: Salads, Italian dishes, pizza, eggplant, mozzarella, parmesan, and fontina cheese.

From: Tuscany, Italy

Made by: Poliziano

www.carlettipoliziano.com

Shoofly
Shiraz

This wine is juicy and spicy, with some berry flavor.
A great easy-going wine.

We found it for $8.98

| LIGHT-BODIED | MEDIUM-BODIED | FULL-BODIED |

Great with: Casual food, including pizza, pasta, sausage, fajitas,
burritos, and barbeque. Also pairs well with grilled seafood.

From: McLaren Flats, South Australia

Made by: Shoofly

www.shooflywines.com

Yalumba
Patchwork Shiraz

Silky fruit complexity is the key here. Features a great balance of flavors.

We found it for $14.84

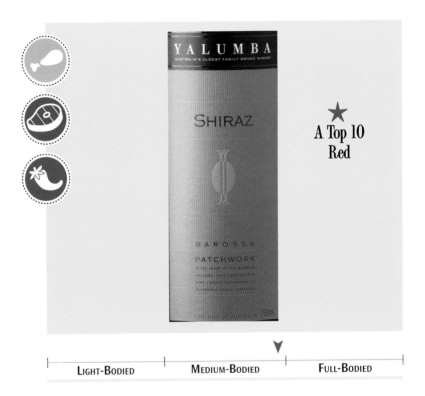

★
A Top 10
Red

Light-Bodied	Medium-Bodied	Full-Bodied

Great with: Spicy dishes including Mexican, Cajun, and barbecue. Also pairs well with grilled meats and chicken.

From: Barossa Valley, South Australia

Made by: Yalumba

www.Yalumba.com

Yalumba Barossa
Shiraz/Viognier

This wine is rich yet not overpowering, with plums and fruit
flavors, and some spice. A perfect blend.

We found it for $5.99

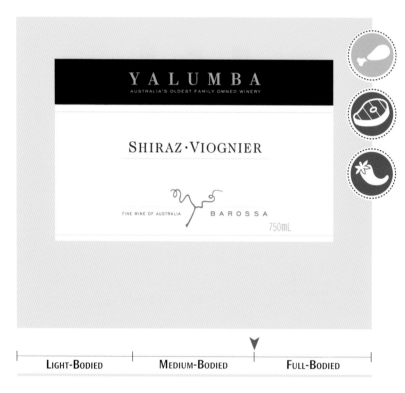

LIGHT-BODIED	MEDIUM-BODIED	FULL-BODIED

Great with: Steak and mushroom pie, hamburgers, lamb chops,
barbecue, and ribs.

From: Barossa Valley, South Australia

Made by: Yalumba

www.Yalumba.com

The Laughing Magpie Shiraz/Viognier

This wine has hints of fruit and spices. It is a great find and value, you can't go wrong with this vineyard!

We found it for $15

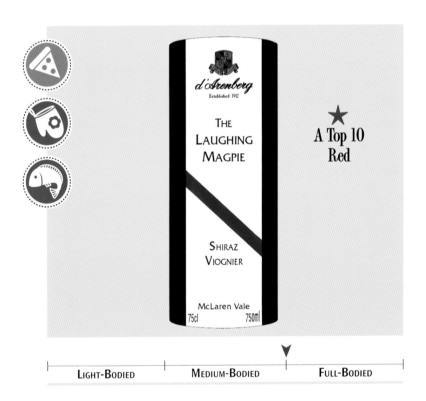

| LIGHT-BODIED | MEDIUM-BODIED | FULL-BODIED |

Great with: Casual food, including pizza, pasta, sausage, fajitas, burritos, and barbeque. Also pairs well with grilled seafood.

From: McLaren Vale, South Australia

Made by: d'Arenberg

www.darenberg.com.au

Zonte's Footstep
Shiraz/Viognier

An excellent blend with some spice, pepper, blackberry, and plum tastes. What a joy for the price!

We found it for $13.98

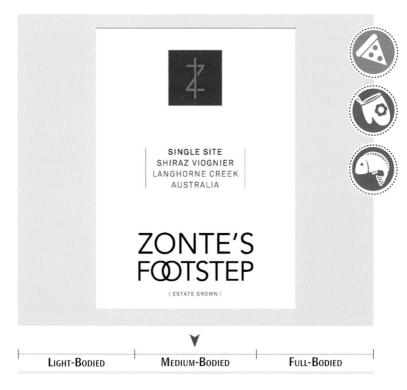

| LIGHT-BODIED | MEDIUM-BODIED | FULL-BODIED |

Great with: Lamb chops, steak, and spicy dishes including Mexican, Cajun, and barbecue.

From: Langhorne Creek, South Australia

Made by: Zonte's Footstep

www.zontesfootstep.com.au

Rosenblum Heritage Clones Petite Sirah

For strong-wine lovers,
yet with balanced flavors and aroma.

We found it for $11.66

| LIGHT-BODIED | MEDIUM-BODIED | FULL-BODIED |

Great with: Chili, smoked prime rib, leg of lamb, perfect with pot roast, and more hearty foods. Also pairs well with grilled seafood.

From: Alameda, Calif.

Made by: Rosenblum Cellars

www.rosenblumcellars.com

Concannon Conservancy
Petite Sirah

You will not believe the price for this
smooth and creamy Sirah!

We found it for $7.99

| LIGHT-BODIED | MEDIUM-BODIED | FULL-BODIED |

Great with: Lamb dishes, sausage, chicken, hamburgers, and
barbeque. Also pairs well with grilled seafood.

From: Livermore, Calif.

Made by: Concannon Vineyard

www.concannonvineyard.com

Vinum Cellars PETS
Petite Sirah

Great wine for the price!
Its finish is generous, fruity, and not too heavy!

We found it for $11.70

| Light-Bodied | Medium-Bodied | Full-Bodied |

Great with: Casual food, including pizza, pasta, sausage, fajitas, burritos, and barbeque. Also pairs well with grilled seafood.

From: Clarksburg, Calif.

Made by: Vinum Cellars

www.vinumcellars.com

Rayun
Syrah

A wine full of blackberry and plum with hints of cherry and a little spice. The price is unbelievable!

We found it for $5.95

Light-Bodied	Medium-Bodied	Full-Bodied

Great with: Casual food, including pizza, pasta, sausage, fajitas, burritos, and barbeque. Also pairs well with grilled seafood.

From: Rapel Valley, Chile

Made by: Rayun

www.northberkeleyimports.com

Fess Parker
Syrah

This wine is robust, full of flavors and spices.
A steal at this price!

We found it for $15.99

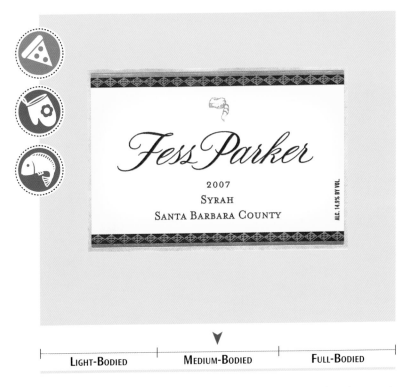

| LIGHT-BODIED | MEDIUM-BODIED | FULL-BODIED |

Great with: Salmon, duck, lamb chops, sausage, fajitas, burritos, and barbeque. Also pairs well with grilled seafood and meats.

From: Los Olivos, Calif.

Made by: Fess Parker Winery

www.fessparker.com

Zaca Mesa
Syrah

A smoky oak wine with spicy balanced aromas and flavors.
A perfect Syrah!

We found it for $15.93

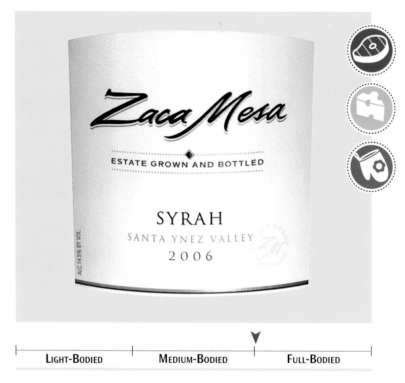

| LIGHT-BODIED | MEDIUM-BODIED | FULL-BODIED |

Great with: Rack of lamb, rosemary or garlic chicken, grilled meats,
  bold cheeses, pizza, and paella.

From: Los Olivos, Calif.

Made by: Zaca Mesa Winery & Vineyards

www.zacamesa.com

Domaine Cazes
Le Canon du Maréchal

An easy-drinking blend—Syrah (50%), Merlot (50%)—with velvety, fruity aromas. Ideal for drinking throughout a meal.

We found it for $9.04

| LIGHT-BODIED | MEDIUM-BODIED | FULL-BODIED |

Great with: Casual food, including pizza, pasta, sausage, fajitas, burritos, and barbeque. Also pairs well with grilled seafood and meat.

From: Rivesaltes, France

Made by: Domaine Cazes

www.cazes-rivesaltes.com

6th Sense
Syrah

This wine is full and rich, with fruit flavors of dark berries, whole plum, and black currant.

We found it for $17.98

| LIGHT-BODIED | MEDIUM-BODIED | ▼ FULL-BODIED |

Great with: Rich or intense-flavored food. Grilled meats, lamb, pot roast, Italian dishes, Moo Shu chicken, hamburgers, and heavy cheeses.

From: Lodi, Calif.

Made by: Michael~David Winery

www.lodivineyards.com

E. Guigal
Côtes du Rhône Rouge

A rich yet smooth wine, round, and racy!
Blends Syrah (50%), Grenache (40%), and Mourvédre (10%).

We found it for $6.98

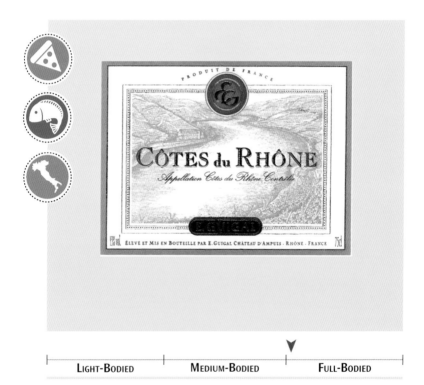

LIGHT-BODIED	MEDIUM-BODIED	▼ FULL-BODIED

Great with: Casual food, including pizza, pasta, sausage, fajitas,
burritos, and barbeque. Also pairs well with grilled seafood.

From: Côtes du Rhône, France

Made by: E. Guigal

www.guigal.com

Mas des Bressades
Cuvée Tradition Rouge

This Syrah/Grenache blend is fresh and ripe with some fruit flavor, yet powerful and pure.

We found it for $10.19

Light-Bodied	Medium-Bodied	Full-Bodied

Great with: All meats, chicken with stir-fry, meatballs with pasta, game, seafood, paella, and Italian dishes.

From: Rhône Valley, France

Made by: Mas des Bressades

www.masdesbressades.com

Domaine
St. Jacques d'Albas

An excellent blend—Syrah (60%), Grenache (20%), and
Carignan (20%)—well balanced, smooth, and spicy.

We found it for $15

LIGHT-BODIED	MEDIUM-BODIED	FULL-BODIED

Great with: Rich or intense-flavored food. Grilled meats, lamb, pot
roast, Italian dishes, Chinese-style shredded beef, Moo Shu pork.

From: Languedoc, France

Made by: Domaine St. Jacques d'Albas

www.chateaustjacques.com

Montes Alpha
Syrah

The perfect blend of Syrah (90%), Cabernet Sauvignon (7%), and Viognier (3%); spicy and full of flavor that lingers.

We found it for $15.89

| Light-Bodied | Medium-Bodied | Full-Bodied |

Great with: Mexican, Cajun and barbecue dishes, spicy chicken, pizza, and grilled shrimp.

From: Santa Cruz, Chile

Made by: Apalta Winery and Vineyards Viña Montes

www.monteswines.com

Petite Petit

A red table wine (85% Sirah, 15% Petit Verdot) that is smooth and silky. A bargain for the price!

We found it for $14.99

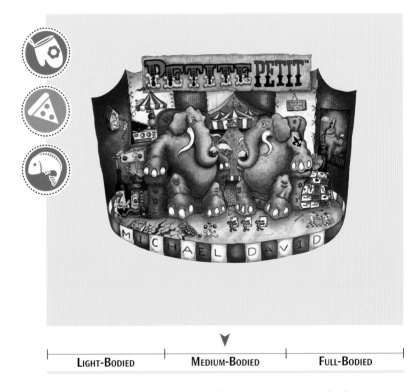

| LIGHT-BODIED | MEDIUM-BODIED | FULL-BODIED |

Great with: Hearty fare such as mixed sausage ragu or barbecue. This spicy wine goes well with casual food, including pizza, pasta, sausage, fajitas or burritos. Also pairs well with grilled seafood.

From: Lodi, Calif.

Made by: Michael~David Winery

www.lodivineyards.com

Valdehermoso
Crianza

One of the great value wines of Spain. This Tempranillo wine has a hint of fruit flavors and a nice long, lingering taste.

We found it for $18.75

LIGHT-BODIED	MEDIUM-BODIED	FULL-BODIED

Great with: Grilled meats, lamb, pork, Italian dishes, Chinese-style meats, cheeses, paella, and hamburgers.

From: Ribera del Duero, Spain

Made by: Valdehermoso

www.zachys.com

Boutari Naoussa

This Greek red table wine is sweet, yet has spices and mint.
A pleasure to drink!

We found it for $11.99

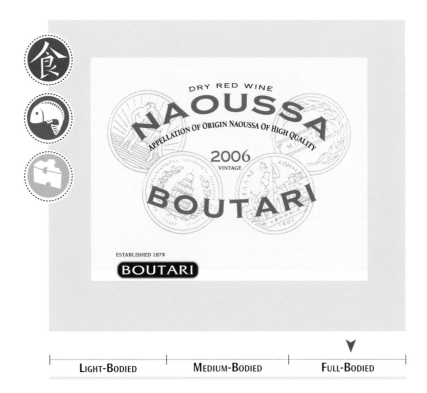

LIGHT-BODIED	MEDIUM-BODIED	FULL-BODIED

Great with: Thai, Chinese and other Asian and Indian dishes. Smoked
fish works well and it can be good with Cheshire, Colby, Edam,
gouda, and Monterey Jack cheeses.

From: Thessaloniki, Greece

Made by: J. Boutari & Son S.A.

www.boutari-wines.com

Goats Do Roam

An excellent blended red table wine, with some fruit flavors and a smooth finish.

We found it for $6.99

| LIGHT-BODIED | MEDIUM-BODIED | FULL-BODIED |

Great with: Grilled seafood, smoky dishes like barbeque, bacon, ribs, light pastas, and baked ham.

From: South Africa

Made by: Goats Do Roam Wine Co.

www.goatsdoroam.com

Ménage à Trois

The perfect red table wine.
It is silky, soft, and pleasant to drink.

We found it for $7.49

LIGHT-BODIED | MEDIUM-BODIED | FULL-BODIED

Great with: Grilled seafood, smoky dishes like barbeque, bacon, ribs,
light pastas, and baked ham.

From: Napa Valley, Calif.

Made by: Folie a' Deux

www.folieadeux.com

Open Range
Proprietary Red Blend

Tastes of plum and black currant with a silky, balanced core.
The perfect wine for party or dinner!

We found it for $18

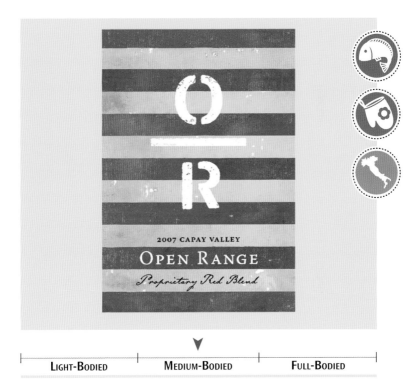

| LIGHT-BODIED | MEDIUM-BODIED | FULL-BODIED |

Great with: Grilled seafood, hamburgers, steaks, pastas, lasagna.

From: Yolo County, Calif.

Made by: Casey Flat Ranch

www.caseyflatranch.com

Joel Gott
Zinfandel

This full-bodied Zinfandel has great taste with a bit of berry flavor, but spicy, with nice pepper taste.

We found it for $12.99

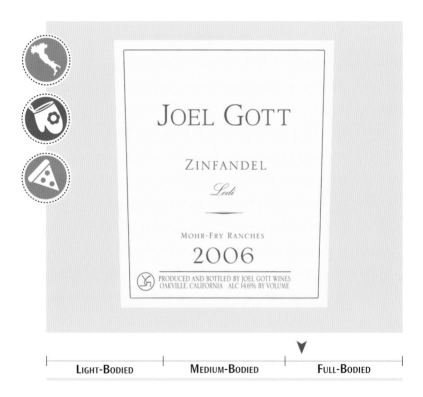

| | LIGHT-BODIED | MEDIUM-BODIED | FULL-BODIED |

Great with: More intensely flavored foods including Italian dishes, barbeque, grilled seafood, pizza, burgers, pastas, and grilled meats.

From: St. Helena, Calif.

Made by: Joel Gott

www.gottwines.com

Relativity
Quantum Reserve

A Zinfandel with smooth, fruit, and pepper flavors.
Very easy to drink.

We found it for $15.98

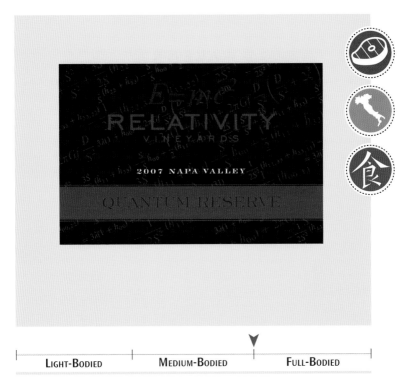

| LIGHT-BODIED | MEDIUM-BODIED | FULL-BODIED |

Great with: Grilled meats, lamb, pot roast, Italian dishes, Chinese-
style meats and pizza, and hamburgers.

From: St. Helena, Calif.

Made by: Relativity Vineyards

www.relativityvineyards.com

Ravenswood
Zinfandel

Ravenswood makes the perfect Zin. A balance of berries and plums, with lingering spice. Can't beat the price!

We found it for $8.99

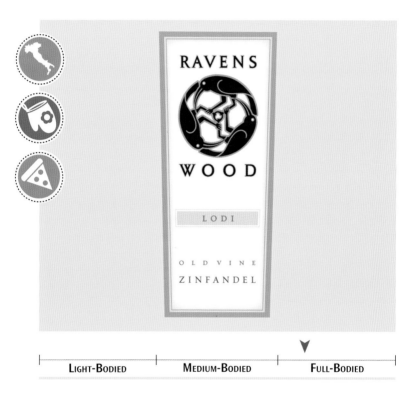

| LIGHT-BODIED | MEDIUM-BODIED | ▼ FULL-BODIED |

Great with: More intensely flavored foods including Italian dishes, barbeque, grilled seafood, pizza, burgers, pasta, and grilled meats.

From: Sonoma, Calif.

Made by: Ravenswood Winery

www.ravenswoodwinery.com

Rodney Strong
Zinfandel

A nice Zin that is firm, well balanced and a with hint of spices.
Excellent and a steal!

We found it for $18.99

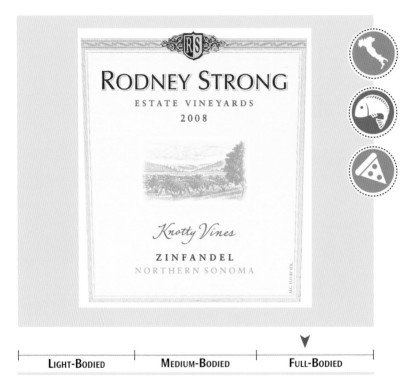

LIGHT-BODIED	MEDIUM-BODIED	FULL-BODIED

Great with: Barbeque, sausages, chili, pizza, burgers, pastas, grilled
meats, spicy-flavored meats, and hearty foods.

From: Healdsburg, Calif.

Made by: Rodney Strong Vineyards

www.rodneystrong.com

Seven Deadly Zins
Zinfandel

A well-balanced Zin, filled with flavors,
including raspberry, cinnamon, and black pepper.

We found it for $9.99

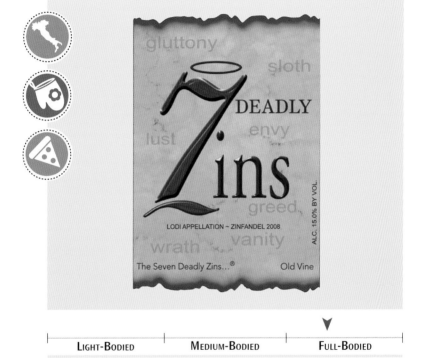

LIGHT-BODIED	MEDIUM-BODIED	FULL-BODIED

Great with: More intensely flavored foods including Italian dishes,
barbeque, grilled seafood, pizza, burgers, pastas, and grilled
meats.

From: Lodi, Calif.

Made by: Michael~David Winery

www.lodivineyards.com

white WINES

Never refuse to do a kindness unless
the act would work great injury to
yourself, and never refuse to take a
drink — under any circumstances.

— Mark Twain's Notebook

La Cana
Albariño

This wine is 100% Albariño grapes, making it dry,
rich in citrus fruits but not too sweet—very enjoyable.

We found it for $11.99

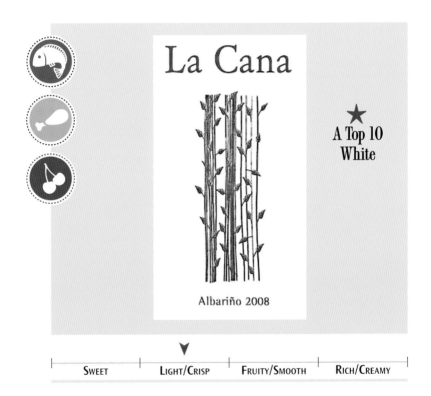

La Cana

Albariño 2008

★
**A Top 10
White**

| SWEET | LIGHT/CRISP | FRUITY/SMOOTH | RICH/CREAMY |

Great with: Shellfish and oysters, Veal Piccata and Chicken Marsala.
It also goes well during cocktail hour, where you may be serving
dried fruits, salsa, and nuts.

From: Spain

Made by: Bodegas La Cana

www.jorge-ordonez.es

Château de Bonhoste
Bordeaux Blanc SEC

A great citrus mix with Sauvignon and butter. Hard to believe a
bottle from Bordeaux could be so inexpensive and so good!

We found it for $12.99

| Sweet | Light/Crisp | Fruity/Smooth | Rich/Creamy |

Great with: Grilled vegetables, salads, grilled salmon, tuna, sole, and
halibut.

From: Bordeaux, France

Made by: Château de Bonhoste

www.chateaudebonhoste.com

Candoni
Moscato

This wine is semi-sparkling with a great fruity flavor,
yet not too sweet.

We found it for $12.49

★
**A Top 10
Sweet**

SWEET	LIGHT/CRISP	FRUITY/SMOOTH	RICH/CREAMY

Great with: Pastries, cakes, desserts, fruit. Excellent dessert wine.

From: Abruzzo, Italy

Made by: Candoni

www.candoniwines.com

Donnafugata
Anthìlia

This Italian wine (a blend of Catarratto and Ansonica grapes) is
smooth and clean with a fruity taste and softness in the mouth.

We found it for $14.99

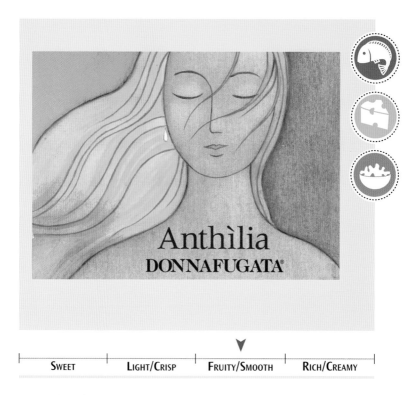

SWEET	LIGHT/CRISP	FRUITY/SMOOTH	RICH/CREAMY

Great with: Lightly smoked fish, crustaceans, and all seafood.
Excellent with tuna salad, eggplant rolls, and stuffed mussels.

From: Marsala, Sicily

Made by: Donnafugata

www.donnafugata.it

Simonnet-Febvre
Chablis

Another great wine out of France. It's a perfect balance, combining full, generous fruit flavors.

We found it for $11.94

| | SWEET | LIGHT/CRISP | FRUITY/SMOOTH | RICH/CREAMY |

Great with: Oysters, Thai dishes, grilled seafood, and fresh salads.

From: Chablis, France

Made by: Simonnet-Febvre

www.simonnet-febvre.com

Adelsheim Chardonnay

A rich, nicely balanced wine, not too "oaky" or sweet.
Nice fruit spice flavors. Just don't tell anyone the price!

We found it for $15.72

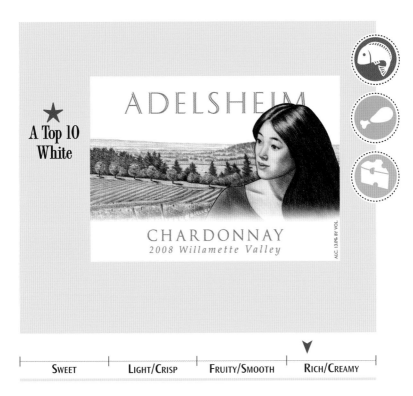

★
A Top 10
White

SWEET	LIGHT/CRISP	FRUITY/SMOOTH	RICH/CREAMY

Great with: Rich foods, cream sauces, and butter. Excellent with
  seafood, veal, chicken, and mild or strong cheeses.

From: Willamette Valley, Ore.

Made by: Adelsheim Vineyard

www.adelsheim.com

Angeline Chardonnay

A nice, crisp wine with pineapple, lemon, peach, and melon flavors throughout.

We found it for $11.34

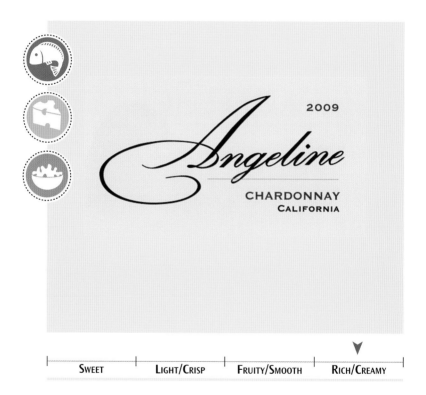

2009

Angeline

CHARDONNAY
CALIFORNIA

SWEET	LIGHT/CRISP	FRUITY/SMOOTH	RICH/CREAMY ▾

Great with: Mango shrimp, lightly spiced halibut with lemon, or petrale sole (flounder), cream sauce pastas, and Caribbean cuisine.

From: Santa Rosa, Calif.

Made by: Martin Ray Winery

www.martinraywinery.com

Babich Hawke's Bay Chardonnay

An abundantly fruity and refreshing wine.
It can be enjoyed from early afternoon on.

We found it for $9.99

| SWEET | LIGHT/CRISP | FRUITY/SMOOTH | RICH/CREAMY |

Great with: Rich foods, cream sauces, and butter. Excellent with seafood, lemon flavored chicken, fettuccine pasta, and veggies.

From: Auckland, New Zealand

Made by: Babich Wines Limited

www.babich.co.nz

Bonterra Chardonnay

This organic wine is rich and creamy in texture.
A hint of oak complements the freshness of fruit and honey.

We found it for $9.99

SWEET	LIGHT/CRISP	FRUITY/SMOOTH	RICH/CREAMY

Great with: Seafood, chicken or veal in cream sauces, Lemon chicken. Excellent with seafood, veal and chicken, mild or strong cheeses, salmon sushi, and California rolls.

From: Mendocino County, Calif.

Made by: Bonterra Vineyards

www.bonterra.com

Calera Central Coast Chardonnay

A fun, full texture yet light tasting wine with citrus and vanilla, touch of toasty oak, and a silky, delicious finish.

We found it for $9.95

| SWEET | LIGHT/CRISP | FRUITY/SMOOTH | RICH/CREAMY |

Great with: Rich foods, cream sauces, and butter. Excellent with seafood (including shellfish), veal, chicken, and mild or strong cheeses.

From: Hollister, Calif.

Made by: Calera Wine Co.

www.calerawine.com

Casa Lapostolle
Cuvée Alexandre Chardonnay

This wine is juicy with lots of ripe fruit flavors, with a lingering creamy finish. Perfect for the price!

We found it for $14.94

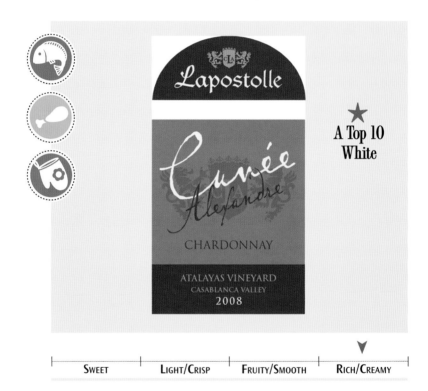

★ A Top 10 White

Sweet	Light/Crisp	Fruity/Smooth	Rich/Creamy

Great with: Medium-seasoned dishes, fried chicken, all seafood, salads, Brie, Gruyere, brick, and Colby cheese.

From: Santa Cruz, Chile

Made by: Casa Lapostolle

www.casalapostolle.com

Chateau Ste. Michelle Chardonnay

Flavors of pineapple and grapefruit, light, and refreshing, with a lingering taste. The perfect food wine!

We found it for $7.98

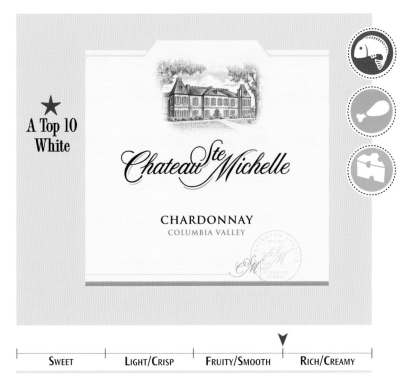

★
A Top 10 White

SWEET	LIGHT/CRISP	FRUITY/SMOOTH	RICH/CREAMY

Great with: Crab cakes, rabbit, all seafood, chicken, and pasta in cream sauces.

From: Woodinville, Wash.

Made by: Chateau Ste. Michelle

www.ste-michelle.com

Chateau Labouré-Roi
Bourgogne-Blanc Chardonnay

Drink to impress! From a prestigious French vineyard,
full and fruity, with a balancing acidity and richness.
This wine is a steal!

We found it for $9.64

| Sweet | Light/Crisp | Fruity/Smooth | Rich/Creamy |

Great with: Rich food, cream sauces and butter. Excellent with
seafood, veal, and chicken. Great with mild and strong cheeses,
and creamy Caesar salad.

From: Meursault, France

Made by: Chateau Labouré-Roi

www.palmbayimports.com

Concannon Conservancy Chardonnay

This wine is rich, dry, creamy, and fresh with flavors of peach, pear, and hints of lemon that balance the fruitiness.

We found it for $10.95

| SWEET | LIGHT/CRISP | FRUITY/SMOOTH | RICH/CREAMY |

Great with: Seafood, crab cakes, chicken in cream sauce, pasta with a heavy sauce, Caribbean cuisine, and oysters.

From: Livermore, Calif.

Made by: Concannon Vineyard

www.concannonvineyard.com

Cycles Gladiator Chardonnay

A buttery and rich Chardonnay, full of taste. A bargain at this price!

We found it for $8.99

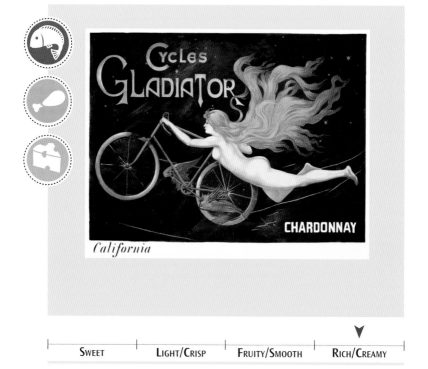

SWEET	LIGHT/CRISP	FRUITY/SMOOTH	RICH/CREAMY

Great with: Seafood, chicken, veal with cream sauce, heavy cheeses, salmon sushi, and California rolls.

From: Napa, Calif.

Made by: Hahn Estates

www.cyclesgladiator.com

Roger Luquet
Clos de Condemine

This Chardonnay has aromas and flavors of fresh apples,
a touch of nutmeg. Perfect for the price!

We found it for $13.75

| SWEET | LIGHT/CRISP | FRUITY/SMOOTH | RICH/CREAMY |

Great with: Excellent with all seafood, lobster, veal, chicken in butter-
based sauces, avocados, and mild or strong cheeses.

From: Macon-Villages, France

Made by: Domaine Roger Luquet

Fess Parker
Chardonnay

An enjoyable wine that is fruity, fresh and crisp,
with a nice aftertaste.

We found it for $8.54

| SWEET | LIGHT/CRISP | FRUITY/SMOOTH | RICH/CREAMY |

Great with: Chicken, crab cakes, all seafood, salads, Brie, Gruyere,
brick, and Colby cheese.

From: Los Olivos, Calif.

Made by: Fess Parker Winery

www.fessparker.com

Foxglove
Chardonnay

This California wine is perfect for dinner, with an aroma of tropical fruit and a crisp flavor.

We found it for $13.29

| SWEET | LIGHT/CRISP | FRUITY/SMOOTH | RICH/CREAMY |

Great with: Creamy Caesar salad, Dijon chicken, poached salmon with hollandaise, veal, chicken, and mild or strong cheeses.

From: Menlo Park, Calif.

Made by: Varner Wine

www.varnerwine.com

Frei Brothers Reserve
Russian River Valley Chardonnay

A nutty and rich wine that finishes
with a silky, full-mouth feel.

We found it for $9.95

| SWEET | LIGHT/CRISP | FRUITY/SMOOTH | RICH/CREAMY |

Great with: Rich foods, cream sauces, and butter. Excellent with
seafood, veal, chicken, and mild or strong cheeses.

From: Healdsburg, Calif.

Made by: Frei Brothers Winery

www.freibrothers.com

Ghost Pines Chardonnay

Your perfect everyday wine!
An elegant, sweet, buttery wine, with toasty vanilla finish.

We found it for $10.99

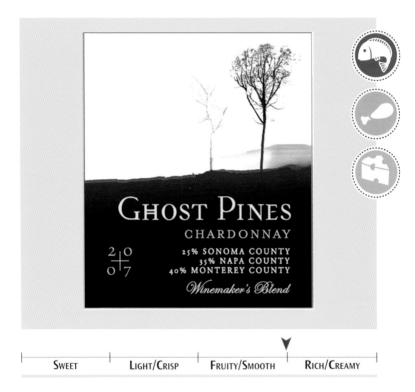

| SWEET | LIGHT/CRISP | FRUITY/SMOOTH | RICH/CREAMY |

Great with: Avocados, salad, all seafood, grilled chicken, pasta in a
    light butter sauce, and mild or strong cheeses.

From: St. Helena, Calif.

Made by: Louis M. Martini Winery

www.ghostpines.com

J. Lohr Riverstone Chardonnay

This wine has an excellent balance of fresh-fruit acidity and tastes of pear and vanilla. A bargain at this price!

We found it for $7.99

SWEET	LIGHT/CRISP	FRUITY/SMOOTH	RICH/CREAMY

Great with: Oven-roasted chicken; lobster stuffed with crab meat, or grilled salmon, Dijon chicken, and Caesar salad.

From: San Jose, Calif.

Made by: J. Lohr Vineyards & Wines

www.jlohr.com

Joel Gott
Chardonnay

A nice dinner wine,
full of crisp citric flavor.

We found it for $12.22

JOEL GOTT

Chardonnay

MONTEREY
2007

CELLARED AND BOTTLED BY JOEL GOTT WINES
OAKVILLE, CALIFORNIA ALC 13.9% BY VOLUME

SWEET	LIGHT/CRISP	FRUITY/SMOOTH	RICH/CREAMY

Great with: Rich foods, cream sauces, and butter. Excellent with seafood, veal, chicken, and mild or strong cheeses. Try with a mixed fruit and nut platter with a selection of cheeses.

From: St. Helena, Calif.

Made by: Joel Gott Wines

www.gottwines.com

Kendall-Jackson Grand Reserve Chardonnay

A standard for many, this wine has tropical fruit flavors
and is oaky, well balanced.

We found it for $13.89

	SWEET	LIGHT/CRISP	FRUITY/SMOOTH	RICH/CREAMY

Great with: Chicken with cream sauces, scallops, crab cakes,
avocados, and sushi.

From: Santa Rosa, Calif.

Made by: Kendall-Jackson

www.kj.com

Louis Jadot Mâcon Villages Chardonnay

This French Chardonnay is another staple for many and is dry, crisp, refreshing, and clean.

We found it for $7.73

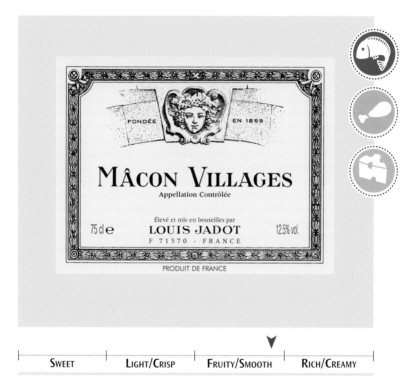

| SWEET | LIGHT/CRISP | FRUITY/SMOOTH | RICH/CREAMY |

Great with: Rich foods, cream sauces, and butter. Excellent with all seafood (including shellfish), veal and chicken, Dijon chicken, Brie, mild or strong cheeses, and Caesar salad.

From: Beaune, France

Made by: Maison Louis Jadot

www.louisjadot.com

Louis Jadot
Pouilly-Fuissé

This well-known Chardonnay is fresh and
full of flavor, with a touch of oak.

We found it for $10.99

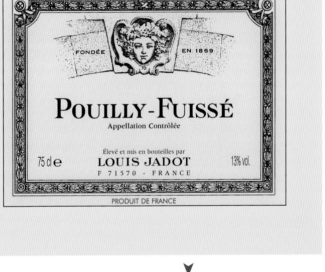

SWEET	LIGHT/CRISP	FRUITY/SMOOTH	RICH/CREAMY

Great with: Seafood, including lobster, scallops, and shrimp. It also
pairs well with cream-based pastas, Caesar salad, and chicken
pot pie.

From: Beaune, France

Made by: Louis Jadot

www.louisjadot.com

Santa Digna
Chardonnay

This Miguel Torres wine is rich in fruit,
balanced with a buttery finish.

We found it for $8.49

| SWEET | LIGHT/CRISP | FRUITY/SMOOTH | RICH/CREAMY |

Great with: Rich foods, cream sauces, and butter. Excellent with
seafood (including shellfish), veal, chicken, and mild or strong
cheeses.

From: Curicó, Chile

Made by: Sociedad Vinicola Miguel Torres S.A.

www.migueltorreschile.com

Plantagenet Omrah
Un-Oaked Chardonnay

Great tasting and juicy, with citrus flavors throughout the wine.

We found it for $12.99

	SWEET	LIGHT/CRISP	FRUITY/SMOOTH	RICH/CREAMY

Great with: Oysters and grilled fish, scallops, mixed seafood salad, grilled chicken, bouillabaisse, and pastas with cream sauce.

From: Mount Barker, Western Australia

Made by: Plantagenet Wines

www.plantagenetwines.com

Simi Sonoma County Chardonnay

Intense flavors that are well balanced—fruit, spice, and butter. This is a staple in many homes.

We found it for $15.97

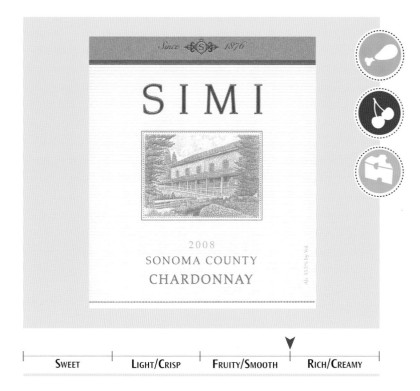

SWEET	LIGHT/CRISP	FRUITY/SMOOTH	RICH/CREAMY

Great with: Mushroom risotto, crab cakes, and roast chicken. Try with a mixed fruit and nut platter featuring a selection of cheeses.

From: Healdsburg, Calif.

Made by: Simi Winery

www.simiwinery.com

Santa Barbara Winery Chardonnay

This Chardonnay has intense fruit flavors and is nicely balanced. A favorite of many.

We found it for $10.99

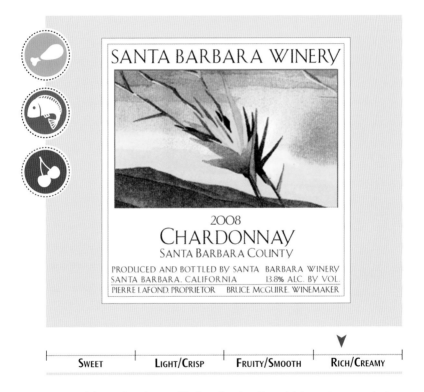

| | SWEET | LIGHT/CRISP | FRUITY/SMOOTH | RICH/CREAMY |

Great with: Crab cakes, grilled seafood, Dijon chicken, Caesar salad, and pasta alfredo.

From: Santa Barbara, Calif.

Made by: Santa Barbara Winery

www.sbwinery.com

Smoking Loon
Chardonnay

An easy-to-drink Chardonnay with nice fruit flavors,
yet rich and smooth.

We found it for $6.99

SWEET | LIGHT/CRISP | FRUITY/SMOOTH | RICH/CREAMY

Great with: Grilled chicken, Caesar salad, pasta in cream sauce, and
poached salmon with hollandaise.

From: Sonoma, Calif.

Made by: Don Sebastiani & Sons

www.donandsons.com

Sterling Chardonnay

This Chardonnay has rich flavors of fruit and spice, and is well balanced. A great Sterling for the price!

We found it for $14.92

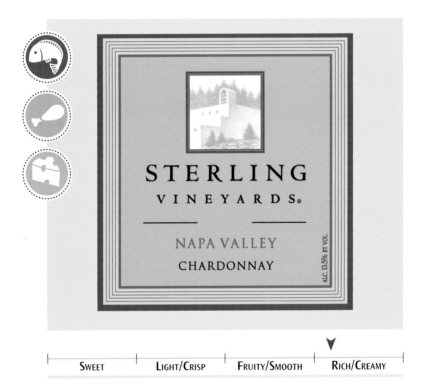

SWEET	LIGHT/CRISP	FRUITY/SMOOTH	RICH/CREAMY

Great with: Rich foods, cream sauces, and butter. Excellent with seafood (including shellfish), veal, chicken, and mild or strong cheeses.

From: Calistoga, Calif.

Made by: Sterling Vineyards

www.sterlingvineyards.com

Trevor Jones
Virgin Chardonnay

This rich wine is complex, with incredible long-lasting taste. You will not believe the price!

We found it for $8.99

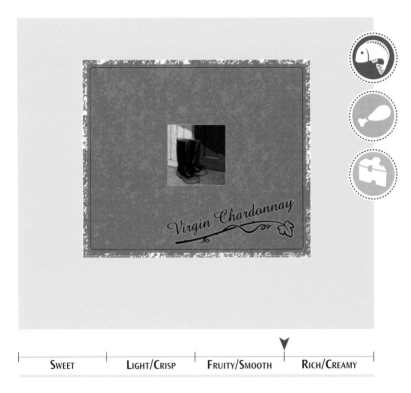

| SWEET | LIGHT/CRISP | FRUITY/SMOOTH | RICH/CREAMY |

Great with: Grilled chicken, Caesar salad, fettuccine alfredo, all seafood, and cheeses.

From: Lyndoch, South Australia

Made by: Kellermeister

www.kellermeister.com.au

Jean-Jacques Vincent Pouilly-Fuissé Marie-Antoinette Chardonnay

This Chardonnay has clean crisp taste,
with a little hint of toast.

We found it for $14.27

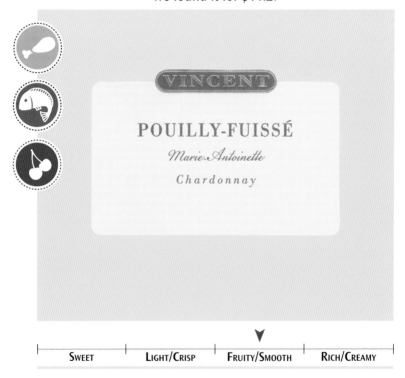

	SWEET	LIGHT/CRISP	FRUITY/SMOOTH	RICH/CREAMY

Great with: Roast chicken, turkey sandwich, sea bass, pasta in a light cream sauce, and goat cheese salad. Try with a mixed fruit and nut platter.

From: Pouilly-Fuissé, France

Made by: Jean-Jacques Vincent Winery

www.chateau-fuisse.fr

Wyatt
Chardonnay

This great Chardonnay is clean, fresh, and fruity.
You can't beat the price!

We found it for $9.49

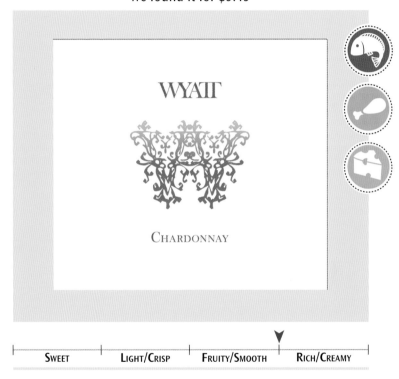

| SWEET | LIGHT/CRISP | FRUITY/SMOOTH | RICH/CREAMY |

Great with: Rich foods, cream sauces and butter. Excellent with seafood, all shellfish, veal, chicken, and mild or strong cheeses.

From: Oakville, Calif.

Made by: Polaner Selections

www.polanerselections.com

Yalumba Eden Valley Chardonnay

This wine—with citrus flavors and some light oak—
has the perfect balance.

We found it for $12.90

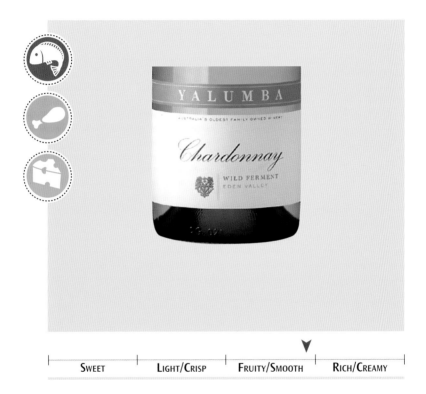

SWEET	LIGHT/CRISP	FRUITY/SMOOTH	RICH/CREAMY

Great with: Fish based risotto. Excellent with grilled cod, halibut, swordfish, and duck with fruit glaze.

From: Angaston, South Australia

Made by: Yalumba

www.yalumba.com

Arrogant Frog
Chardonnay Viognier

What a nice surprise for the price! This wine is light for a
Chardonnay/Viognier blend. Fun, smooth, dry, and silky.

We found it for $7.49

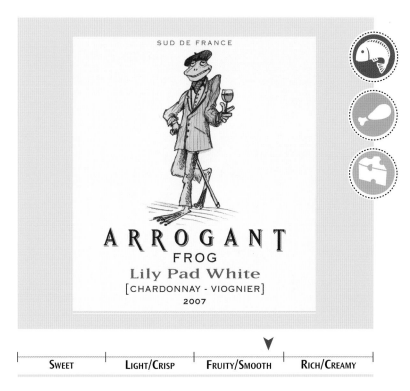

Sweet	Light/Crisp	Fruity/Smooth	Rich/Creamy

Great with: Spicy tuna roll, spicy crab roll, goat cheese salad, chicken
  in cream sauce and all seafood.

From: Languedoc, France

Made by: Domaines Paul Mas

www.arrogantfrog.fr

MAN Vintners
Chenin Blanc

A nice light taste, crisp and refreshing with
some fruit flavors of melons and peaches.
Perfect for a sunset sail.

We found it for $6.99

SWEET	LIGHT/CRISP	FRUITY/SMOOTH	RICH/CREAMY

Great with: Grilled seafood, "raw bar" (raw oysters, shrimp cocktail,
king crab legs), salads, Mediterranean food, and Asian fare.

From: South Africa, coastal region

Made by: MAN Vintners

www.manvintners.co.za

Vinum Cellars
Chenin Vio

An enjoyable wine (a blend of Chenin Blanc-Viognier)
from California. Great for the price, with a nice balance
of apricot and peach flavors.

We found it for $9.37

| Sweet | Light/Crisp | Fruity/Smooth | Rich/Creamy |

Great with: Curry chicken, goat cheese salad, sun-dried tomato salad,
and fresh Thai food.

From: Oakville, Calif.

Made by: Vinum Cellars

www.vinumcellars.com

Feudi di San Gregorio
Fiano di Avellino

This Italian wine is dry and has
elegant florals and freshness. A favorite of many!

We found it for $17.99

Sweet	Light/Crisp	Fruity/Smooth	Rich/Creamy

Great with: Oysters, all fish (with sauces or grilled), roasted chicken, and grilled vegetables.

From: Campania, Italy

Made by: Feudi di San Gregorio

www.feudi.it/en

Latium Morini
Campo le Calle Soave

A rarer Garganega wine that is sure to impress.
Rich, ripe with tastes of yellow peaches. Sweet on the palate.

We found it for $11

| SWEET | LIGHT/CRISP | FRUITY/SMOOTH | RICH/CREAMY |

Great with: Asian cuisine (Japanese, Chinese, Indian, Thai), soups, grilled fish, oysters, stir-fry, and curry.

From: Vento, Italy

Made by: Latium

Latium Morini
Soave

A refreshing Garganega wine that is bright and
floral with excellent clarity and freshness.

We found it for $14

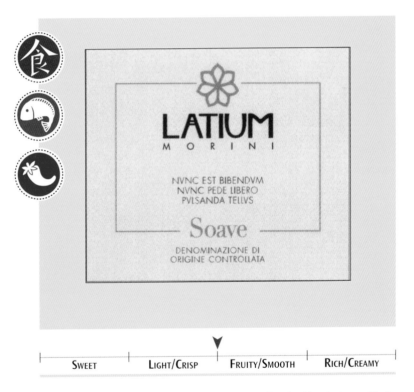

SWEET	LIGHT/CRISP	FRUITY/SMOOTH	RICH/CREAMY

Great with: Curry chicken, shrimp satay, beef teriyaki, stir-fry, grilled
fish, and grilled seafood.

From: Vento, Italy

Made by: Latium

Anselmi
San Vincenzo

A blend of 80% Garganega, 5% Soave Trebbiano, 15% Chardonnay. It is dry and fresh, with a nice fruit balance.

We found it for $9.99

Sweet	Light/Crisp	Fruity/Smooth	Rich/Creamy

Great with: Grilled fish, grilled shrimp, oysters, chicken teriyaki, and mixed green salads.

From: Monteforte d'Alpone, Italy

Made by: Roberto Anselmi

www.robertoanselmi.com

Brandborg
Gewürztraminer

A dry to semi-sweet blend of tropical fruit,
well balanced with full and rich flavor!

We found it for $12.94

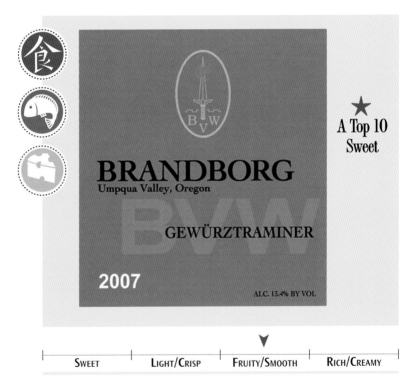

★
A Top 10
Sweet

| SWEET | LIGHT/CRISP | FRUITY/SMOOTH | RICH/CREAMY |

Great with: Asian cuisine (Japanese, Chinese, Indian, Thai). Smoked
fish, stir-fry, curry chicken, chicken and seafood pad thai.

From: Elkton, Ore.

Made by: Brandborg Vineyard & Winery

www.brandborgwine.com

Boutari
Moschofilero

A well-balanced, intense wine,
followed by a nice light citrus flavor.

We found it for $11.39

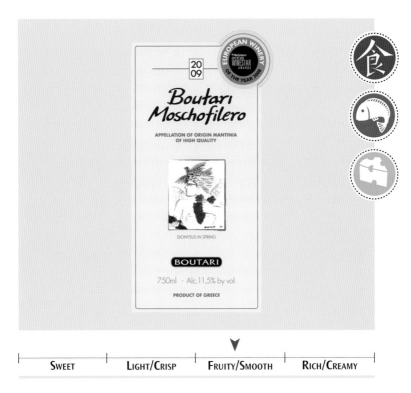

| SWEET | LIGHT/CRISP | FRUITY/SMOOTH | RICH/CREAMY |

Great with: Chicken satay, mixed Greek salad, shellfish, and
  Mediterranean salad.

From: Thessaloniki, Greece

Made by: J. Boutari & Son S.A.

www.boutari-wines.com

Altanuta
Pinot Grigio

This wine is so refreshing! It is creamy with tastes of fruit, dried apricot, and slight spice, with a long finish.

We found it for $10.22

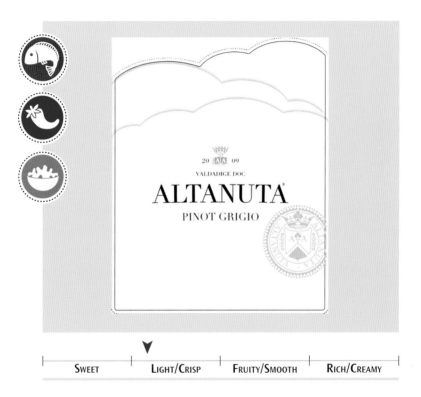

| SWEET | LIGHT/CRISP | FRUITY/SMOOTH | RICH/CREAMY |

Great with: Grilled seafood, seafood pastas/salad, Mediterranean, Greek salad, roasted chicken, and artichoke dip.

From: Valdadige, Italy

Made by: Altanuta

www.altanutawine.com

Barefoot Cellars
Pinot Grigio

Light-bodied and flavorful. Everyone knows about it and you cannot complain about the price of this one!

We found it for $6.99

SWEET	LIGHT/CRISP	FRUITY/SMOOTH	RICH/CREAMY

Great with: Grilled seafood, Mediterranean and Asian cuisine, Prosciutto and melon, and chicken salad.

From: Modesto, Calif.

Made by: Barefoot Cellars

www.barefootwine.com

Bottega Vinaia Trentino Pinot Grigio

This wine is delightful, dry, and crisp with a lingering finish.

We found it for $12.95

| SWEET | LIGHT/CRISP | FRUITY/SMOOTH | RICH/CREAMY |

Great with: Grilled seafood, Mediterranean or Asian cuisine, Spanakopita, artichoke dip, light pasta salad, seafood, and pad thai.

From: Trento, Italy

Made by: Bottega Vinaia

www.palmbay.com

Cavit
Pinot Grigio

This inexpensive wine is a staple for many at a party on a
summer day. It is light and crisp with fruit flavors.

We found it for $9.99

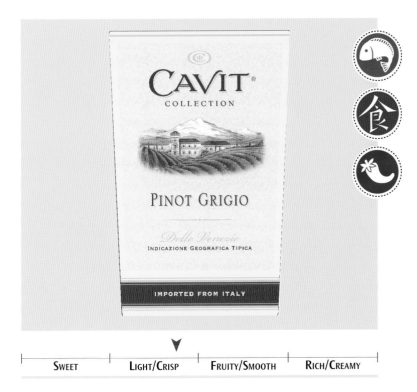

| SWEET | LIGHT/CRISP | FRUITY/SMOOTH | RICH/CREAMY |

Great with: Grilled seafood, Mediterranean or Italian dishes, Tex Mex
and Asian cuisine, quesadilla, fresh seafood, and hummus dip.

From: Trento, Italy

Made by: Cavit Collection

www.cavitcollection.com

Benton Lane
Pinot Gris

This wine has a crisp apple taste. It is light and refreshing and perfect for a sunset.

We found it for $13.95

★
A Top 10
White

SWEET	LIGHT/CRISP	FRUITY/SMOOTH	RICH/CREAMY

Great with: Grilled seafood, oysters and mussels, moo shu shrimp, shrimp kabob, and Tex Mex and Asian cuisine. Pairs well with parmesan cheese and feta cheese.

From: Monroe, Ore.

Made by: Benton Lane Winery

www.benton-lane.com

Erath
Pinot Gris

This wine exhibits tastes of tropical fruit and lemon, and is well balanced. A fun wine for a summer night.

We found it for $13.99

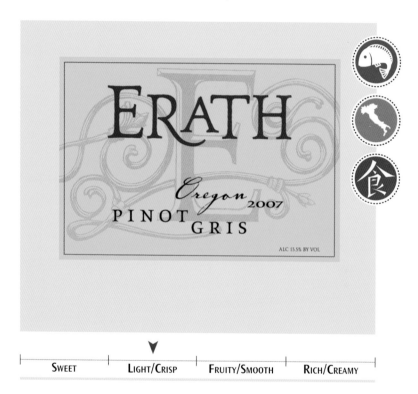

| SWEET | LIGHT/CRISP | FRUITY/SMOOTH | RICH/CREAMY |

Great with: Pad thai, chicken kabob, shellfish, trout in a lemon sauce, light spicy food, and Mediterranean or Italian dishes. Pairs well with assorted nuts and cheeses.

From: Dundee, Ore.

Made by: Erath Winery

www.Erath.com

Gallo Family Vineyards
Sonoma Pinot Gris

A nice, inexpensive Pinot Gris that tastes of peach,
fresh pear, and green apple—well balanced.
No one will believe the price!

We found it for $8.99

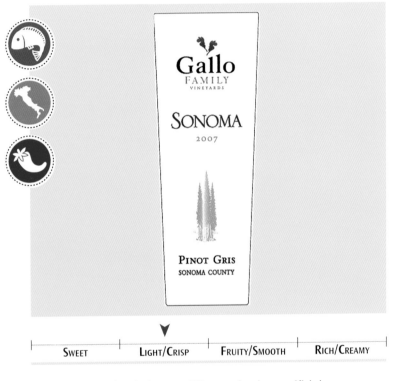

SWEET	LIGHT/CRISP	FRUITY/SMOOTH	RICH/CREAMY

Great with: Greek salad, quesadillas, seafood, swordfish in capers
and lemon sauce, and shrimp satay.

From: Healdsburg, Calif.

Made by: Gallo Family Vineyards

www.gallosonoma.com

J Wine
Pinot Gris

This crisp wine has hints of margarita lime.
Recently publicized in numerous magazines as one of the best
Pinot Gris. Our wine tasters agreed.

We found it for $13.95

★
**A Top 10
White**

SWEET | LIGHT/CRISP | FRUITY/SMOOTH | RICH/CREAMY

Great with: Spicy Asian, all seafood, turkey, chicken pad thai, tacos, and guacamole.

From: Healdsburg, Calif.

Made by: J Vineyards & Winery

www.jwine.com

Sineann
Pinot Gris

A wonderful Pinot Gris coming out of Oregon, with great texture and fruit flavor. Quite refreshing on a hot day.

We found it for $14.99

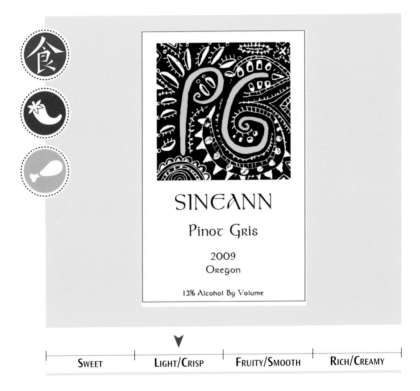

SWEET	LIGHT/CRISP	FRUITY/SMOOTH	RICH/CREAMY

Great with: Salmon roll, spicy tuna sushi, light pasta, chicken Marsala, artichoke dip, and Asian dishes.

From: Newberg, Ore.

Made by: Medici/Sineann Winery

www.sineann.com

Bonterra
Riesling

This organically grown wine is a balance of crisp acidity and a slight sweetness. Very refreshing!

We found it for $14.92

| SWEET | LIGHT/CRISP | FRUITY/SMOOTH | RICH/CREAMY |

Great with: Enchiladas, chicken pad thai, shrimp curry, vegetable stir-fry, lox, and cream cheese.

From: Mendocino, Calif.

Made by: Bonterra Vineyards

www.bonterra.com

Brandborg
Riesling

A dry wine with a cleansing hint of sweet fruit
balanced by the acidity.

We found it for $12.94

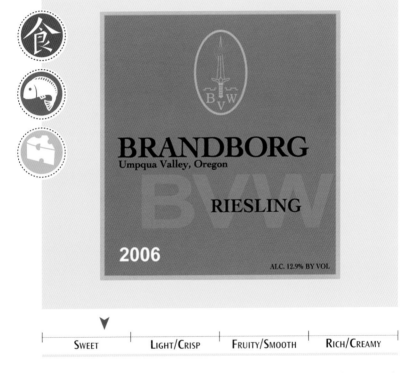

| SWEET | LIGHT/CRISP | FRUITY/SMOOTH | RICH/CREAMY |

Great with: Burritos, spicy tuna rolls, egg rolls, tandoori chicken, and
garlic shrimp.

From: Elkton, Ore.

Made by: Brandborg Vineyard & Winery

www.brandborgwine.com

Chateau Ste. Michelle Eroica Riesling

A favorite of many Riesling lovers, it has a taste of mandarin orange and sweet lime aromas and flavors, fruity, and crisp.

We found it for $11.98

★
A Top 10
Sweet

| SWEET | LIGHT/CRISP | FRUITY/SMOOTH | RICH/CREAMY |

Great with: Smoked salmon, shrimp tempura, chicken sukha, quesadilla, and pad thai.

From: Woodinville, Wash.

Made by: Chateau Ste. Michelle

Dr. Loosen
Riesling

The perfect Riesling. Fruity, crisp, and very refreshing to drink.
Don't tell anyone the price! They will not believe you.

We found it for $7.95

★
**A Top 10
Sweet**

▼			
SWEET	LIGHT/CRISP	FRUITY/SMOOTH	RICH/CREAMY

Great with: Thai, Chinese, and other Asian and Indian dishes.
   Smoked fish works well and it can be good with Colby, Gouda, and
   Monterey Jack cheeses.

From: Bernkastel/Mosel, Germany

Made by: Dr. Loosen

www.drloosen.com

Hermann J. Wiemer
Dry Riesling

A Riesling wine with honey, crisp and rich taste, and nicely balanced, creating an impressive finish.

We found it for $14.95

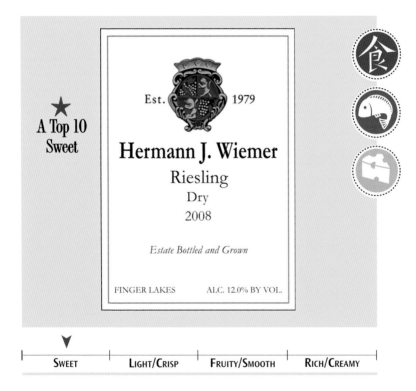

Great with: Nova lox, spicy appetizers, pork roast, and smoked trout. Pairs well with Indian and Asian foods.

From: Starkey, N.Y.

Made by: Hermann J. Wiemer Vineyard

www.wiemer.com

Leasingham
Magnus Riesling

Smooth and sweet with lemony citrus.
Perfect and refreshing.

We found it for $10.99

★
A Top 10
Sweet

| Sweet | Light/Crisp | Fruity/Smooth | Rich/Creamy |

Great with: Chow Mein, smoked salmon, garlic shrimp, turkey, and
mixed salad.

From: Clare Valley, South Australia

Made by: Leasingham Wines

www.leasingham-wines.com.au

Leeuwin Estate Art Series Riesling

A refreshing wine with lemon, grapefruit, and lime flavor. Clean and crisp.

We found it for $13.99

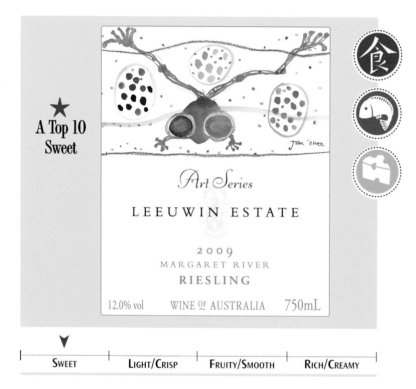

★
A Top 10 Sweet

Art Series

LEEUWIN ESTATE

2009
MARGARET RIVER
RIESLING

12.0% vol   WINE OF AUSTRALIA   750mL

| SWEET | LIGHT/CRISP | FRUITY/SMOOTH | RICH/CREAMY |

Great with: Oysters, shrimp tempura, pad thai, Greek salad, lox and cream cheese.

From: Margaret River, Western Australia

Made by: Leeuwin Estate Winery

www.leeuwinestate.com.au

Pacific Rim
Riesling

One of the favorites from all wine tastings. This Riesling has bright crispness and subtle sweetness. The perfect Riesling.

We found it for $8.94

★
A Top 10 White

| SWEET | LIGHT/CRISP | FRUITY/SMOOTH | RICH/CREAMY |

Great with: Nice with spicy or rich food, pad thai, enchiladas, shrimp curry, and veggie stir-fry.

From: Columbia Valley, Wash.

Made by: Pacific Rim

www.rieslingrules.com

Pacific Rim
Sweet Riesling

Perfect for those who love sweet wine.
This has flavors of pineapple and peach.

We found it for $8.94

★
A Top 10
Sweet

SWEET	LIGHT/CRISP	FRUITY/SMOOTH	RICH/CREAMY

Great with: Jerk chicken, spring rolls, Szechwan chicken, sticky rice, or as an after-dinner drink.

From: Columbia Valley, Wash.

Made by: Pacific Rim

www.rieslingrules.com

Pacific Rim Organic Riesling

This Riesling is another favorite. Perfect for organic lovers. It is nicely balanced and sweet.

We found it for $11.90

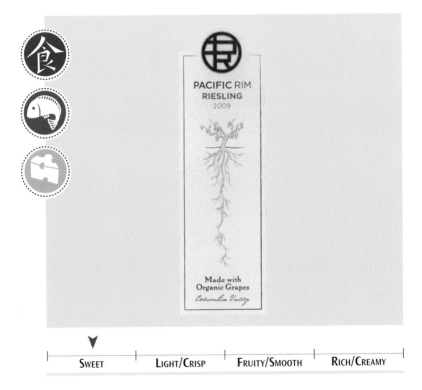

SWEET	LIGHT/CRISP	FRUITY/SMOOTH	RICH/CREAMY

Great with: Foods with lots of flavor and spicy food: smoked fish, stir fry, lox and cream cheese, and assorted cheeses including Cheshire, Colby, Edam, Gouda, and Monterey Jack.

From: Columbia Valley, Wash.

Made by: Pacific Rim

www.rieslingrules.com

SeaGlass
Riesling

A nice, refreshing sweet wine, with a sweet
fruit flavor that is crisp and light.

We found it for $9.99

SWEET	LIGHT/CRISP	FRUITY/SMOOTH	RICH/CREAMY

Great with: Spicy ribs, curry lobster, smoked salmon, Greek salad,
Thai, Chinese, and Asian and Indian dishes.

From: St. Helena, Calif.

Made by: SeaGlass

www.seaglasswines.com

Paul et Jean-Marc Pastou Sancerre

A fantastic Sancerre. Refreshing with juicy citrus flavors and lighter on the body. One of the best Sancerres for the price.

We found it for $17.99

Les Boucaults

Vieilles   *Vignes*

SANCERRE
APPELLATION SANCERRE CONTROLEE
WHITE LOIRE WINE
Paul et Jean-Marc PASTOU
S.C.E.V.
Propriétaires Récoltants
NET CONTENTS 750 ML   Sury-en-Vaux SANCERRE (CHER)   ALCOHOL 13 % BY VOL.
Mise en bouteille au domaine   CONTAINS SULFITES
PRODUCT OF FRANCE

IMPORTED BY : MICHAEL SKURNIK WINES, SYOSSET, NY

| SWEET | LIGHT/CRISP | FRUITY/SMOOTH | RICH/CREAMY |

Great with: Seafood including shellfish, snapper, trout, raw oysters, sushi, halibut and tuna. Caesar salad, mild cheeses, Mexican and Asian cuisine also pair well.

From: Sury en Vaux, France

Made by: Paul et Jean-Marc Pastou Winery

www.skurnikwines.com

Boutari
Santorini

A dry white, ripe, and intense wine. Has a juicy pear flavor and richness to balance the acidity. A treat from Greece.

We found it for $14.71

SWEET	LIGHT/CRISP	FRUITY/SMOOTH	RICH/CREAMY

Great with: Thai, Chinese, and other Asian and Indian dishes. Smoked fish works well and it can be good with Cheshire, Colby, Edam, Gouda, and Monterey Jack cheeses.

From: Thessaloniki, Greece

Made by: J. Boutari & Son S.A.

www.boutariwines.com

Seventy-Five Wine Co.
Sauvignon Blanc

This wine has citrus, tropical fruit flavors, and a touch of lemongrass. Light and juicy, perfect for a sunny day!

We found it for $14.99

SWEET	LIGHT/CRISP	FRUITY/SMOOTH	RICH/CREAMY

Great with: Seafood, snapper, trout, raw oysters, halibut, tuna, crudite, chicken salad, artichoke spinach dip, and seven-layer dip.

From: St. Helena, Calif.

Made by: Tuck Beckstoffer Wines

www.75wine.com

Babich Marlborough Sauvignon Blanc

This is a lovely wine with good aromas of herbs and some citrus taste.

We found it for $9.67

| SWEET | LIGHT/CRISP | FRUITY/SMOOTH | RICH/CREAMY |

Great with: Tzatziki and hummus dip, sushi, all seafood, deviled eggs, and chef salad.

From: Auckland, New Zealand

Made by: Babich Wines Limited

www.babich.co.nz

Bonterra
Sauvignon Blanc

This organically grown wine is crisp, with slight tropical fruit flavors. Perfect for sailing into the sunset!

We found it for $14.92

| Sweet | Light/Crisp | Fruity/Smooth | Rich/Creamy |

Great with: All seafood, cheese plate of Brie, Monterey Jack, Gouda, chevre, grapes and nuts, chef salad, and grilled chicken.

From: Mendocino, Calif.

Made by: Bonterra Vineyards

www.bonterra.com

Henri Bourgeois Petit Bourgeois Sauvignon Blanc

This wine is like a gorgeous summer day. It is crisp, fruity, zesty, and well balanced.

We found it for $10.99

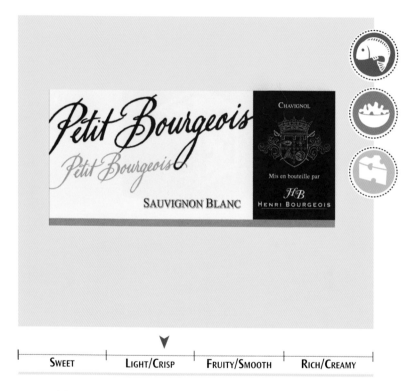

| SWEET | LIGHT/CRISP | FRUITY/SMOOTH | RICH/CREAMY |

Great with: Crab cakes, all seafood, egg salad, salad with grilled chicken, and crudite.

From: Vin de Pays, France

Made by: Domaine Henri Bourgeois

www.henribourgeois.com

Box O' Birds
Sauvignon Blanc

A fantastic, fun, exuberant Sauvignon Blanc
with tangy grapefruit and lime flavors.

We found it for $12.99

SWEET	LIGHT/CRISP	FRUITY/SMOOTH	RICH/CREAMY

Great with: All seafood, chef salad, tzatziki and hummus dip, veggie
burgers, and lox and cream cheese.

From: Cromwell, New Zealand

Made by: Prophet's Rock Vineyard Ltd.

J. Lohr Carol's Vineyard Sauvignon Blanc

Light and crisp with flavors of grapefruit and tropical fruit. Perfect for a day of sailing.

We found it for $13.95

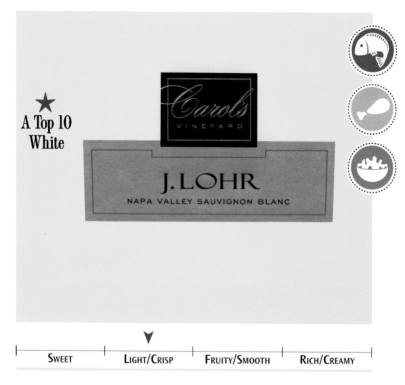

★ A Top 10 White

| SWEET | LIGHT/CRISP | FRUITY/SMOOTH | RICH/CREAMY |

Great with: Seven-layer bean dip, deviled eggs, chicken salad, all seafood, and fried chicken.

From: San Jose, Calif.

Made by: J. Lohr Vineyards & Wines

www.jlohr.com

Kendall-Jackson Vintner's Reserve Sauvignon Blanc

A favorite of many, this crisp wine has a mix of lemon lime. And you can not believe the price!

We found it for $8.49

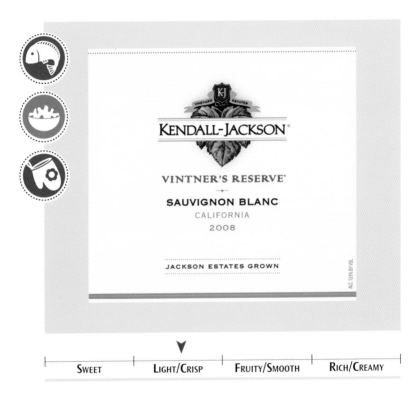

| SWEET | LIGHT/CRISP | FRUITY/SMOOTH | RICH/CREAMY |

Great with: Veggie burgers, cheese platter with cheddar Jack, Brie, parmesan, and Gruyere, chicken salad, and all seafood.

From: Sonoma County, Calif.

Made by: Kendall-Jackson

www.kj.com

Kim Crawford Marlborough Sauvignon Blanc

Our choice for wine at the beach, this is sweet, with a nice passion fruit and lime taste—fresh and zesty.

We found it for $7.95

A Top 10 White

| SWEET | LIGHT/CRISP | FRUITY/SMOOTH | RICH/CREAMY |

Great with: Chef salad, tomato salads, meatless dishes, crudite, artichoke or spinach dip, and all seafood.

From: Huapai, Auckland, New Zealand
Made by: Kim Crawford Wines

www.kimcrawfordwines.co.nz

Momo
Sauvignon Blanc

This crisp and dry wine is rich with ripe tropical
fruit and grapefruit flavors.

We found it for $12.88

| SWEET | LIGHT/CRISP | FRUITY/SMOOTH | RICH/CREAMY |

Great with: Waldorf salad, Greek salad, crudite, all seafood, and
shrimp cocktail.

From: Marlborough, New Zealand

Made by: Seresin Estate

www.momowine.com

Nautilus
Sauvignon Blanc

A delicious wine with hints of melon and grapes.
Some say zingy and zesty.

We found it for $12.17

| SWEET | LIGHT/CRISP | FRUITY/SMOOTH | RICH/CREAMY |

Great with: Egg salad, tuna salad, grilled chicken, veggie burgers and all seafood.

From: Renwick, Marlborough, New Zealand

Made by: Nautilus Estate

www.nautilusestate.com

Open Range
Sauvignon Blanc

Perfect for a summer day.
Fresh, crisp, refreshing flavor with hints of citrus fruits.

We found it for $15

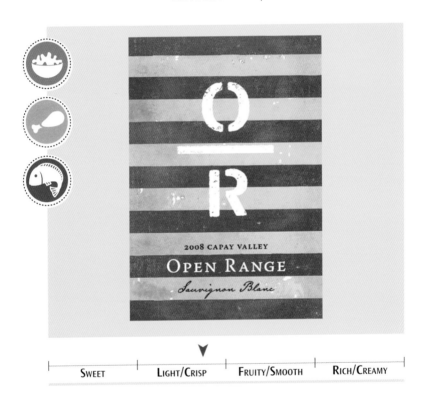

SWEET	LIGHT/CRISP	FRUITY/SMOOTH	RICH/CREAMY

Great with: Caesar salad, mild cheese, vegetarian dishes, all shellfish, roasted chicken, and broiled snapper or trout.

From: Capay Valley or Yolo County, Calif.

Made by: Casey Flat Ranch

www.caseyflatranch.com

Plantagenet Omrah Sauvignon Blanc

This wine has vibrant fruit flavors,
with a clean finish. Fun to drink anytime!

We found it for $13.49

| | SWEET | LIGHT/CRISP | FRUITY/SMOOTH | RICH/CREAMY |

Great with: Seafood (including shellfish), snapper, trout, raw oysters,
   sushi, halibut, tuna, quesadilla, and Waldorf salad.

From: Mount Barker, Western Australia

Made by: Plantagenet Wines

Oyster Bay
Sauvignon Blanc

Zesty refreshment with lime and grapefruit flavors,
this wine is a cool breeze on a hot day.

We found it for $7.99

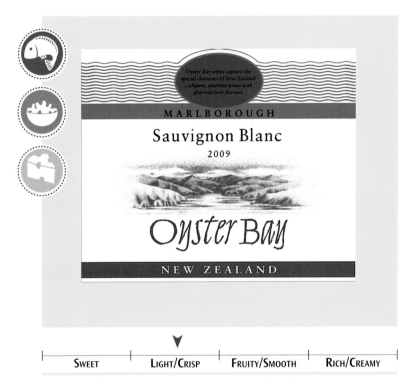

| SWEET | LIGHT/CRISP | FRUITY/SMOOTH | RICH/CREAMY |

Great with: Tuna fish salad, all seafood, crudite, veggie burgers, chef
salad, and spinach dip.

From: Auckland, New Zealand

Made by: Oyster Bay Wines New Zealand Ltd.

www.oysterbaywines.com

Rodney Strong Charlotte's Home Sauvignon Blanc

A typical fresh and lively Sauvignon Blanc
with full crisp and light fruit flavors.

We found it for $8.99

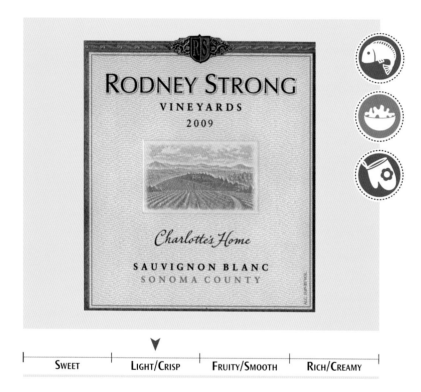

SWEET	LIGHT/CRISP	FRUITY/SMOOTH	RICH/CREAMY

Great with: All seafood, sushi, deviled eggs, grilled chicken over
   mixed greens, artichoke hearts, and hearts of palm.

From: Healdsburg, Calif.

Made by: Rodney Strong Vineyards

Russian Jack
Sauvignon Blanc

This wine displays all the right characteristics of a
Sauvignon Blanc with crisp fruit and strong citrus.

We found it for $13.99

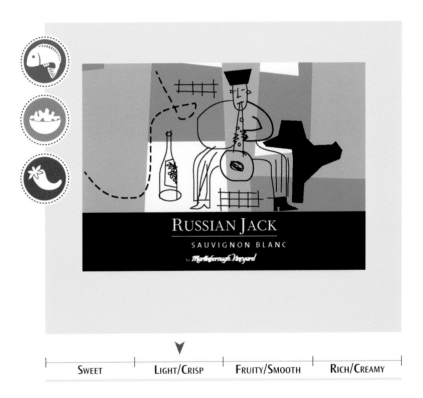

SWEET	LIGHT/CRISP	FRUITY/SMOOTH	RICH/CREAMY

Great with: Smoked salmon, tzatziki and hummus dip, seven layer
bean dip, and fried chicken.

From: Waipara Valley, New Zealand

Made by: Martinborough Vineyard

www.martinborough-vineyard.co.nz

Santa Barbara Winery Sauvignon Blanc

A wonderful Sauvignon Blanc with tropical fruit accent, light, and zesty. An amazing find for the price!

We found it for $6.51

| Sweet | Light/Crisp | Fruity/Smooth | Rich/Creamy |

Great with: Light or spicy foods, grilled veggies, citrus chicken, salads, steamed crabs, lox and cream cheese, and pad thai.

From: Santa Barbara, Calif.

Made by: Santa Barbara Winery

Sean Minor
Sauvignon Blanc

A crisp wine with flavors of pear,
fig and melon—well balanced.

We found it for $10.24

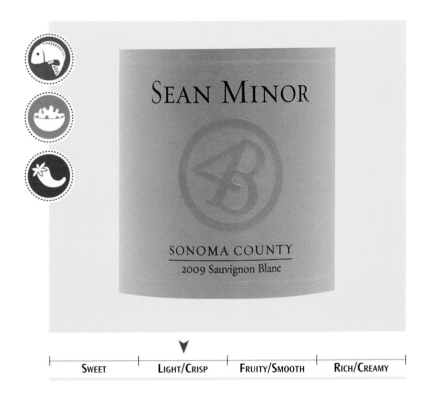

SWEET	LIGHT/CRISP	FRUITY/SMOOTH	RICH/CREAMY

Great with: Snapper, trout, raw oysters, sushi, halibut, tuna, Caesar
salad, mild cheeses, and Mexican and Asian cuisine.

From: Napa, Calif.

Made by: Sean Minor Wines

www.4bearswinery.com

Shaw and Smith
Sauvignon Blanc

A perfect all-round wine!
It is crisp, fresh and lively with fruit flavors.

We found it for $17.99

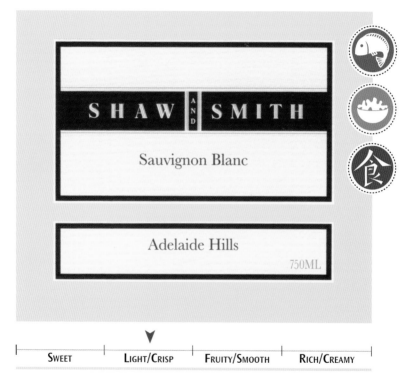

SWEET	LIGHT/CRISP	FRUITY/SMOOTH	RICH/CREAMY

Great with: Seven-layer bean dip, quesadilla, walnuts, grapes,
   cheddar Jack, Gouda, all shellfish, and raw bar.

From: Balhannah, South Australia

Made by: Shaw + Smith Wines

www.shawandsmith.com

Sterling
Sauvignon Blanc

A refreshing Sauvignon Blanc that has crisp flavors,
including grapefruit, melon, and pineapple.

We found it for $10.99

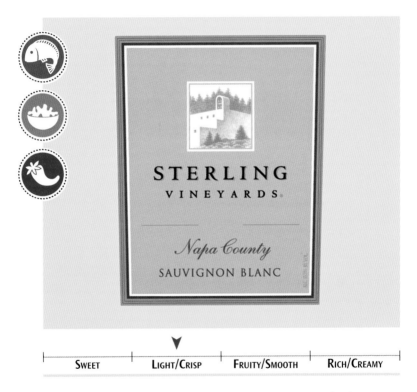

| SWEET | LIGHT/CRISP | FRUITY/SMOOTH | RICH/CREAMY |

Great with: All seafood, crab cakes, grilled chicken on mixed greens,
and goat cheese salad.

From: Calistoga, Calif.

Made by: Sterling Vineyards

www.sterlingvineyards.com

Thelema
Sauvignon Blanc

This wine is full of juicy melon and grapefruit flavor
and has a wonderful dry finish.

We found it for $13.99

SWEET	LIGHT/CRISP	FRUITY/SMOOTH	RICH/CREAMY

Great with: Tuna fish salad, egg salad, crudite, pad thai, and lox and
cream cheese.

From: Stellenbosch, South Africa

Made by: Thelema Mountain Vineyards

www.thelema.co.za

Veramonte
Sauvignon Blanc

A wine with citrus, melon, and herb flavors.
You can't beat the price!

We found it for $8.94

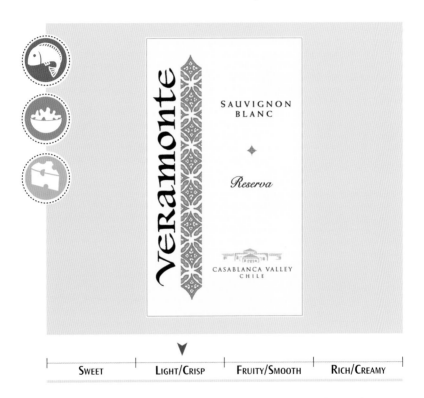

| SWEET | LIGHT/CRISP | FRUITY/SMOOTH | RICH/CREAMY |

Great with: All seafood, chef salad, tomato salad, crudite, and artichoke or spinach dip.

From: Casablanca, Chile

Made by: Veramonte Winery

www.veramonte.com

Villa Maria
Sauvignon Blanc

This rich wine is juicy, with great crisp flavors of fruit.
A great all-round wine!

We found it for $14.99

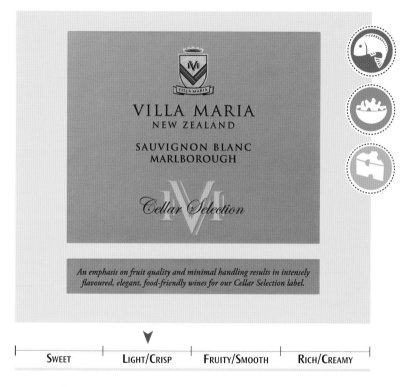

| SWEET | LIGHT/CRISP | FRUITY/SMOOTH | RICH/CREAMY |

Great with: Turkey sandwich, Waldorf salad, shrimp cocktail, oysters,
and meatless dishes.

From: Marlborough, New Zealand

Made by: Villa Maria Estate

www.villamaria.co.nz

Cadaretta
SBS

This is a dry, clean, and crisp blend of Sauvignon Blanc/
Semillon with a creamy texture.

We found it for $16.99

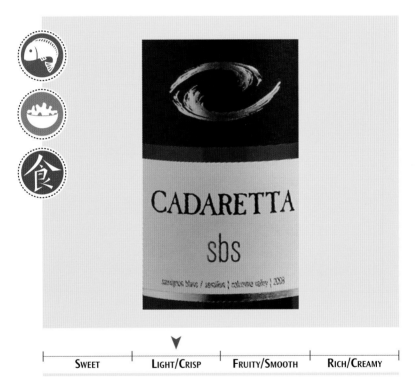

| SWEET | LIGHT/CRISP | FRUITY/SMOOTH | RICH/CREAMY |

Great with: Tuna, sole, fried calamari, and citrus salad. Wonderful
with desserts, cakes, and brownies!

From: Walla Walla, Wash.

Made by: Cadaretta Wines

www.cadaretta.com

Brokenwood
Semillon

This crisp and fresh wine has the perfect balance
of fruits and a touch of citrus.

We found it for $14.95

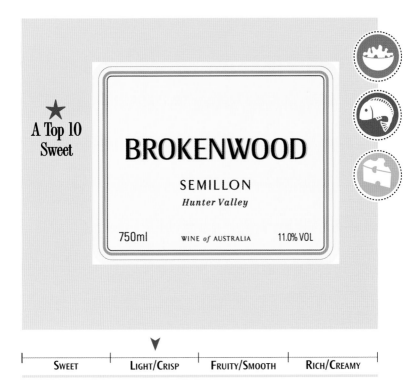

A Top 10
Sweet

BROKENWOOD

SEMILLON
Hunter Valley

750ml WINE *of* AUSTRALIA 11.0% VOL

SWEET	LIGHT/CRISP	FRUITY/SMOOTH	RICH/CREAMY

Great with: Grilled vegetables and seafood, fried chicken, chicken
salad, biscotti, and apple pie. Fun with rice pudding.

From: Hunter Valley, Australia

Made by: Brokenwood

www.brokenwood.com.au

Anselmi
Soave

Crisp, dry, and fresh, with flavors of citrus, pear, and grapefruit. A perfect Italian white.

We found it for $15

SWEET	LIGHT/CRISP	FRUITY/SMOOTH	RICH/CREAMY

Great with: Lobster salad, clams, flounder, seafood salad, and roast chicken.

From: Monteforte d'Alpone, Italy

Made by: Roberto Anselmi

www.robertoanselmi.com

Crios de Susana Balbo Torrontes

This wine is a favorite from Crios. It is full of flavor, juicy, and dry. Perfect on a summer day.

We found it for $9.95

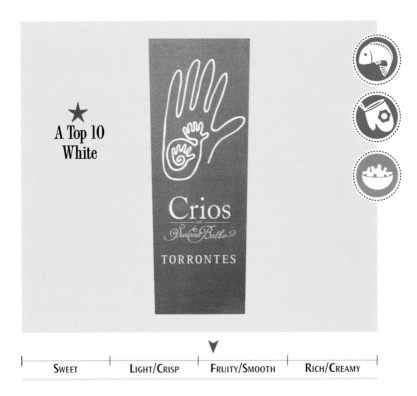

★
A Top 10
White

| SWEET | LIGHT/CRISP | FRUITY/SMOOTH | RICH/CREAMY |

Great with: Trout, scallops, grilled mahi mahi, crabs (steamed), smoked salmon, Thai salads, and Waldorf chicken salad.

From: Mendoza, Argentina

Made by: Domino Del Plata

www.dominiodelplata.com.ar

Tariquet Classic
Ugni Blanc/Colombard

A unique blend of Ugni Blanc (70%) and Colombard (30%). It is delicious, dry, and light, with touches of fruit.

We found it for $8.34

| SWEET | LIGHT/CRISP | FRUITY/SMOOTH | RICH/CREAMY |

Great with: Seafood salad, all shellfish, sushi, lox and cream cheese, chicken salad, and crab cakes.

From: Southwest-Armagnac, France

Made by: Domaine du Tariquet

www.robertkacherselections.com

Feudi della Medusa Albithia Vermentino

Easy drinking, this wine is filled with
loads of tropical fruits, citrus, and spices.

We found it for $16.52

SWEET	LIGHT/CRISP	FRUITY/SMOOTH	RICH/CREAMY

Great with: Seafood. Excellent with white fish, fried calamari, and
   Mediterranean foods. Also try tuna and egg salad.

From: Sardinia, Italy

Made by: Feudi della Medusa

www.feudidellamedusa.it

Colli di Serrapetrona
Vernaccia Nera Collequanto

What a find! This Italian wine is full-bodied, not too sweet,
but not too dry. It has sweet spices and is soft to drink.

We found it for $15

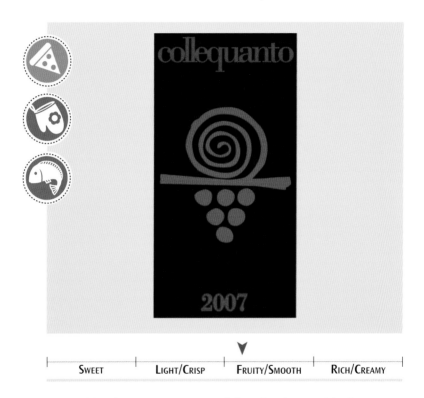

SWEET	LIGHT/CRISP	FRUITY/SMOOTH	RICH/CREAMY

Great with: Pizza, pasta, sausages, fajitas, burritos, and barbeque.
This wine also pairs well with grilled seafood.

From: Le Marche, Italy

Made by: Colli di Serrapetrona

www.collidiserrapetrona.it

Contra' Soarda
Vespaiolo

A crisp, floral white with flavors of ripe apricots,
peaches, hazelnuts, and minerals.

We found it for $16

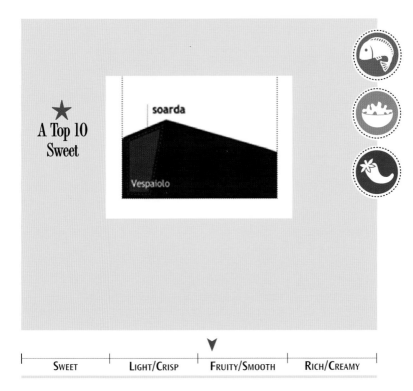

★
**A Top 10
Sweet**

| SWEET | LIGHT/CRISP | FRUITY/SMOOTH | RICH/CREAMY |

Great with: Seafood including shellfish, snapper, trout, raw oysters,
sushi, halibut, and tuna. Cheese plates of goat and Asiago Pressato.
Also try pasta in pesto sauce.

From: Bassano del Grappa, Italy

Made by: Contra' Soarda

www.contrasoarda.it

Rosenblum Cellars
Viognier Kathy's Cuvée

This nice Viognier has hints of tropical fruit and just a touch of toasted oak and vanilla.

We found it for $12.80

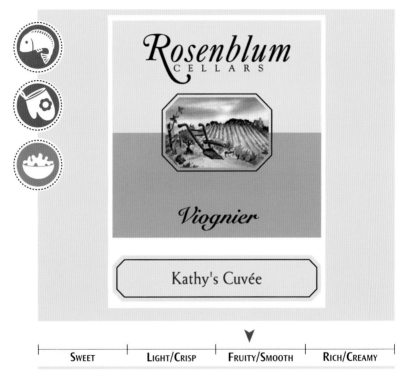

| SWEET | LIGHT/CRISP | FRUITY/SMOOTH | RICH/CREAMY |

Great with: Chicken marsala, grilled swordfish, lobster in cream sauce, white clam chowder, and goat cheese salad.

From: Alameda, Calif.

Made by: Rosenblum Cellars

www.rosenblumcellars.com

E. Guigal
Côtes du Rhône Blanc

Fruity with plenty of richness. A blend of Viognier, Roussanne, Marsanne, Clairette, and Bourboulenc.

We found it for $6.90

SWEET	LIGHT/CRISP	FRUITY/SMOOTH	RICH/CREAMY

Great with: Seafood, swordfish, snapper, trout, egg rolls, chow mein, and pad thai.

From: Côtes du Rhône, France

Made by: E. Guigal

www.guigal.com

Folie a' Deux
Ménage à Trois

Mixing Chardonnay, Muscat, and Chenin Blanc grapes, this very affordable white table wine is rich and creamy, with a perfect mix of citrus and fruit.

We found it for $7.49

| SWEET | LIGHT/CRISP | FRUITY/SMOOTH | RICH/CREAMY |

Great with: Seafood (including shellfish), snapper, trout, raw oysters, sushi, halibut, and tuna. Caesar salad, mild cheeses, Mexican and Asian cuisine also pair well.

From: Napa Valley, Calif.

Made by: Folie a' Deux

www.folieadeux.com

Domaine de la Petite Cassagne
Costières de Nîmes Blanc

This wine is fresh with bright citrus fruit. It is rich and
balanced with flavors of black cherries and chestnuts.
A blend of Rolle (40%) and Grenache Blanc (60%).

We found it for $11.99

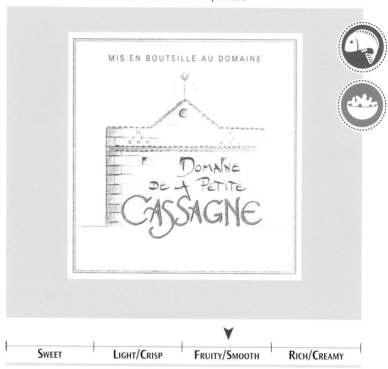

| SWEET | LIGHT/CRISP | FRUITY/SMOOTH | RICH/CREAMY |

Great with: Seafood (including shellfish), snapper, trout, raw oysters,
sushi, halibut, tuna, chef salad, and tuna fish salad.

From: Saint Gilles, France

Made by: Domaine de la Petite Cassagne

www.robertkacherselections.com

Winery Contacts

The 75 Wine Co.
Tuck Beckstoffer Wines
807 St. Helena Highway South,
    Suite One
St. Helena, CA 94574
707-200-4410
www.75wine.com

Adelsheim Vineyard
16800 N.E. Calkins Lane
Newberg, OR 97132
503-538-3652
www.adelsheim.com

www.altanutawine.com
(Located in the Valdadige region,
    in the northeast corner of Italy
    near Austria.)

Arrogant Frog
www.arrogantfrog.fr
(A line of estate-bottled wines
    from the Languedoc region of
    southern France.)
Palm Bay International
301 Yamato Road, No. 1150
Boca Raton, FL 33431
561-362-9642
www.palmbayimports.com

Azienda Agricola
Roberto Anselmi
Via. S. Carlo, 46 37032
Monteforte d'Alpone (VR) Italy
+39 045 7611488
www.robertoanselmi.com

Babich Wines Limited
Babich Road, Henderson
Auckland 0614, New Zealand
Telephone: +64 9 833 7859
www.babichwines.co.nz

Barone Ricasoli S.p.A Agr.
Cantine del Castello di Brolio
53013 Gaiole di Chianti – Siena,
    Italy
+39 0577 7301
www.ricasoli.it

Benton-Lane Winery
P.O. Box 99
23924 Territorial Hwy.
Monroe, OR 97456
541-847-5792
www.benton-lane.com

Blackstone Winery
8450 Sonoma Highway
Kenwood, CA 95452
800-955-9585
www.blackstonewinery.com

Bodegas Condesa de Leganza
Ctra. Madrid - Alicante,
  km. 121.700
45800 Quintanar de la Orden
  – Toledo, Spain
945 60 12 28
www.bodegasleganza.com

Bodegas San Alejandro
Ctra. Calatayud - Cariñena,
  Km. 16,4
50330 Miedes, Zaragoza, Spain
+34 976 892 205
www.san-alejandro.com

Bodegas y Viñedos
Hugo & Eduardo Pulenta S.A.
Gutiérrez 323 (5500) Ciudad.
  Mendoza, Argentina
0054 (261) 420 - 0800
www.pulentaestate.com

Bogle Vineyards
37783 County Road 144
Clarksburg, CA 95612
916-744-1139
www.boglewinery.com

Bonterra Vineyards
2231 McNab Ranch Road
Ukiah, CA. 95482
888-618-0535
www.bonterra.com

Bottega Vinaia
(Family-farmed vineyards in
  northern Italy's Trentino
  region.)
Palm Bay International
301 Yamato Road, No. 1150
Boca Raton, FL 33431
561-362-9642
www.palmbayimports.com

Boutari Wineries
Greekwine.biz, the Greek wine
  portal.
www.boutari-wines.com

Brokenwood Wines PTY Ltd.
401 - 427 McDonalds Road
Pokolbin NSW 2320 Australia
61 02 4998 7559
www.brokenwood.com.au

Cadaretta Winery
1102 Dell Ave.
Walla Walla, WA 99362
509-591-0324
www.cadaretta.com

Calera Wine Co.
11300 Cienega Road
Hollister, CA 95023
Phone: 831-637-9170
www.calerawine.com

Candoni Wines
www.candoniwines.com

Casa Lapostolle
Camino San Fernando a
  Pichilemu, Km 36
Cunaquito, Comuna Sta Cruz,
  Chile
56-72 953 300
www.casalapostolle.com

Castello Di Bossi Spa
Bossi in Chianti - 53019
Castelnuovo Berardenga – Siena,
  Italy
+ 39 0577 35 93 30
www.castellodibossi.it

Catena Zapata
J. Cobos s/n
Agrelo, Luján de Cuyo, Mendoza,
    Argentina
54 261 413 1100
www.catenawines.com

Cavit Collection
(From the Trentino-Alto Adige
    provinces of northern Italy.)
Palm Bay International
301 Yamato Road, No. 1150
Boca Raton, FL 33431
561-362-9642
www.cavitcollection.com

Col D'orcia S.R.L. Societa'
    Agricola
Via Giuncheti - 53024 Montalcino
    – Siena, Italy
+39 0577 80891
www.coldorcia.it

Columbia Crest Winery
Hwy 221, Columbia Crest Drive
Paterson, WA 99345
888-309-9463
www.columbiacrest.com

Concannon Vineyard
4590 Tesla Road
Livermore, CA 94550
800-258-9866
www.concannonvineyard.com

Chateau Ste. Michelle
14111 N.E. 145th St.
Woodinville, WA 98072
800-267-6793
www.ste-michelle.com

d'Arenberg Wineries
Osborn Road
McLaren Vale SA 5171 Australia
+61 8 8329 4888
www.darenberg.com.au

Domaine des Baumard
8, Rue de l'Abbaye
49190 Rochefort-sur-Loire,
    France
02 41 78 70 03
www.baumard.fr

Dominio Del Plata Winery
Cochabamba 7801 Agrelo (5507)
Mendoza, Argentina
+54 261 498 9200
www.dominiodelplata.com.ar

Domaine E. Guigal
69420 Ampuis, France
04 74 56 10 22
www.guigal.com

Donnafugata Winery S.r.l.
Via S. Lipari 18 - 91025 Marsala,
    Sicily
+39 0923 724 245/263
www.donnafugata.it

Dreyfus, Ashby and Co.
630 3rd Ave., Suite 15
New York, NY 10017
212-818-0770,
www.dreyfusashby.com

Earl Vignobles Fournier
Château de Bonhoste
33420 Saint Jean de Blaignac,
    Bordeaux, France
+33 557 84 12 18
www.chateaudebonhoste.com

Ernesto Catena Vineyards
Mendoza, Argentina
+54.11 4331-1251
www.tikalwines.com

Estancia Winery
980 Bryant Canyon Road
Soledad, CA 93960
831-678-7000
www.estanciaestates.com

Fattoria Viticcio S.r.l.
Via San Cresci, 12/A - Greve in
    Chianti, Firenze, Italy
055 854210
www.fattoriaviticcio.com

Fess Parker Winery
6200 Foxen Canyon Road
Los Olivos, CA 93441
800-841-1104
www.fessparker.com

Feudi di San Gregorio
www.feudi.it

Folie à Deux Winery
7481 St. Helena Highway
Oakville, CA 94562
707-944-2565
www.folieadeux.com

Gallo of Sonoma
320 Center St.
Healdsburg, CA 95448
www.gallosonoma.com

Giant Steps / Innocent Bystander
336 Maroondah Hwy
Healesville VIC 3777 Australia
61 (03) 5962 6111
www.innocentbystander.com.au

The Goats Do Roam Wine Co.
P.O. Box 583
Suider-Paarl 7624 South Africa
+27 21 863 2450
www.goatsdoroam.com

Henri Bourgeois
Chavignol 18300 Sancerre,
    France
33 248 785 320
www.henribourgeois.com

Hermann J. Wiemer Vineyard
3692 Route 14
Dundee, NY 14837
607-243-7971
www.wiemer.com

Jan D'Amore Wines
55 Washington St., Suite 312F
Brooklyn, NY 11201
917-257-7994
www.jandamorewines.com

J. Lohr Vineyards & Wines
1000 Lenzen Ave.
San Jose, CA 95126
408-288-5057
www.jlohr.com

Joel Gott Wines
P.O. Box 539
St. Helena, CA 94574
707-963-3365
gottwines.com

Kim Crawford Wines
45 Station Road
Huapai, Auckland, New Zealand
+64 9 412 6666
www.kimcrawfordwines.co.nz

Kendall-Jackson Wine Center
5007 Fulton Road
Fulton, CA 95439
866-287-9818
www.kj.com

Labouré-Roi Wines
Nuits-Saint-George, Burgundy,
    France
Palm Bay International
301 Yamato Road, No. 1150
Boca Raton, FL 33431
561-362-9642
www.palmbayimports.com

La Posta (Argentina)
Vine Connections
415-332-8466
www.lapostavineyards.com

Leasingham Winery
Clare Valley, South Australia
www.leasingham-wines.com.au

Leeuwin Estate Winery
Stevens Road
Margaret River, 6285 Western
    Australia
61 8 9759 0000
www.leeuwinestate.com.au

Loosen Bros. USA Ltd.
20501 S. Tranquility Lane
Oregon City, OR 97045
503-984-3041
www.drloosen.com

MacMurray Ranch
3387 Dry Creek Road
Healdsburg, CA 95448-9740
888-668-7729
www.macmurrayranch.com

Main Street Winery
P.O. Box 248
St. Helena, CA 94574
707-963-3104
www.mainstwinery.com

Maison Louis Jadot
21 rue Eugène Spuller BP 80117
21203 Beaune Cedex, France
+ 33 3 80 22 10 57
www.louisjadot.com

Martin Ray Winery
2191 Laguna Road
Santa Rosa, CA 95401
707-823-2404
www.martinraywinery.com

Medici/Sineann Winery
28005 N.E. Bell Road
Newberg, OR 97132
503-341-2698
www.sineann.com

Michael~David Winery
4580 West Highway 12
Lodi, CA 95242
888-707-WINE
www.lodivineyards.com

MOMO Wines
Marlborough, New Zealand
www.momowine.com

Monte Antico (Tuscany, Italy)
Empson (USA) Inc.
719 Prince St.
Alexandria, VA 22314-3004
703-684-0900
www.monteanticowine.com

Muga Winery
Barrio de la Estación s/n
26200 Haro, La Rioja, Spain
+34 941 31 18 25
www.bodegasmuga.com

Napa Cellars
7481 St. Helena Highway
Oakville, CA 94562
800-535-6400
www.napacellars.com

Nautilus Estate
12 Rapaura Road
Renwick, Marlborough, New
    Zealand
+64 3572 6008
www.nautilusestate.com

North Berkeley Wine
1601 Martin Luther King Jr. Way
Berkeley, CA 94709
800-266-6585
www.northberkeleyimports.com

Oyster Bay Wines New Zealand
    Limited
Level 1, 10 Viaduct Harbour Ave.
Auckland 1010 New Zealand
+64 9 359 7300
www.oysterbaywines.com

Polaner Selections
19 N. Moger Ave.
Mount Kisco, NY 10549
914-244-0404
www.polanerselections.com

Poliziano Azienda Agricola
(Located in the province of Siena
    in southern Tuscany.)
Palm Bay International
48 Harbor Park Drive
Port Washington, NY 11050
516-802-4707
www.carlettipoliziano.com

Plantagenet Wines
Lot 45 Albany Hwy
Mount Barker, Western Australia
    6324
+ 61 8 9851 3111
www.plantagenetwines.com

Ravenswood Winery
18701 Gehricke Road
Sonoma, CA 95476
707-938-1960
www.ravenswoodwinery.com

Roagna Azienda Agricola i
    Paglieri
Paglieri 9, 12050 Barbaresco,
    Italy
+39.0173.635109
www.roagna.com

Rodney Strong Vineyards
11455 Old Redwood Highway
Healdsburg, CA 95448
800-678-4763
www.rodneystrong.com

Rosenblum Cellars
Alameda Winery & Tasting Room
2900 Main St., Suite 1100
Alameda, CA 94501
510-865-7007
www.rosenblumcellars.com
Pacific Rim
www.rieslingrules.com

Ruffino S.r.l. (Tuscany, Italy)
www.ruffino.it

Santa Barbara Winery
202 Anacapa St.
Santa Barbara, CA 93101
805-963 3633
www.sbwinery.com

Santa Margherita
Terlato Wines International
www.SantaMargherita.us

SeaGlass Wine Co.
St. Helena, Calif.
www.seaglasswines.com

Sean Minor Wines
1370 Trancas St., No. 327
Napa, CA 94558
707-226-1414
www.4bearswinery.com

Sella & Mosca (Sardinia, Italy)
Palm Bay International
48 Harbor Park Drive
Port Washington, NY 11050
516-802-4707
www.sellaandmosca.com

Shaw + Smith Pty Ltd.
Jones Road
Balhannah, South Australia 5242
+61 8 83980500
www.shawandsmith.com

Shoofly Wines
295 Douglas Gully Road
McLaren Flats, South Australia
www.shooflywines.com

Simi Winery
16275 Healdsburg Ave.
Healdsburg, CA 95448
800-746-4880
www.simiwinery.com

Sterling Vineyards
1111 Dunaweal Lane
Calistoga, CA 94515-9635
707-942-3344
www.sterlingvineyards.com

Thelema Mountain Vineyards
   (Pty) Ltd.
Helshoogte Pass, Stellenbosch,
   South Africa
+27 (0) 21 885 1924
www.thelema.co.za

Trinchero Family Estates
277 St. Helena Hwy (Hwy. 29)
   South
St. Helena, CA 94574
800-967-4663
www.tfewines.com

Vendemmia International Wines
www.vendemmia.ca

Veramonte Winery
Ruta 68, km 66.
Casablanca, Chile
56 32 2329924
www.veramonte.com

Vignobles Alain Jaume et Fils
Domaine Grand Veneur
Route de Châteauneuf du Pape
   84100 Orange, France
04.90.34.68.70
www.domaine-grand-veneur.com

Vignobles de Larose
St. Laurent, Medoc, Bordeaux,
    France
www.chateau-larose-trintaudon.fr

Villa Maria Estate Auckland
118 Montgomerie Road
Mangere, Manukau, New
    Zealand
+64 9 255 0660
www.villamaria.co.nz

Viña Cobos
Costa Flores y Ruta 7, Perdriel,
Luján de Cuyo – Mendoza,
    Argentina
+ 54 261 4790130
www.vinacobos.com

Vinum Cellars
135 Camino Dorado, Suite 6
Napa, CA 94558
707-254-8313,
www.vinumcellars.com

www.wineanorak.com
A site created by Jamie Goode,
    a London-based writer who is
    currently wine columnist with
    the UK's Sunday Express.

Yalumba
Eden Valley Road
Angaston SA 5353 Australia
www.Yalmuba.com

Zaca Mesa Winery & Vineyards
6905 Foxen Canyon Road
Los Olivos, CA 93441
805-688-9339
www.zacamesa.com

Zonte's Footstep
P.O. Box 353, Main Road
McLaren Vale, South Australia
    5171 Australia
+61 (0)8 8556 2457
www.zontesfootstep.com.au

Elyse's Top 10
Whites, Reds and Sweet

Top 10 Whites

1. J Wine Pinot Gris *(p. 185)*
2. J. Lohr Carol's Vineyard Sauvignon Blanc *(p. 205)*
3. La Cana Albariño *(p. 134)*
4. Crios de Susana Balbo Torrontes *(p. 225)*
5. Adelsheim Chardonnay *(p. 139)*
6. Chateau Ste. Michelle Chardonnay *(p. 145)*
7. Casa Lapostolle Cuvée Alexandre Chardonnay *(p. 144)*
8. Pacific Rim Riesling *(p. 194)*
9. Kim Crawford Marlborough Sauvignon Blanc *(p. 207)*
10. Benton Lane Pinot Gris *(p. 182)*

Top 10 Reds

1. Crios de Susana Balbo Malbec *(p. 69)*
2. The Laughing Magpie Shiraz/Viognier *(p. 108)*
3. Estancia Pinot Noir *(p. 89)*
4. Ex-Libiris Cabernet Sauvignon *(p. 43)*
5. Innocent Bystander Pinot Noir *(p. 91)*
6. Kendall-Jackson Vintner's Reserve Merlot *(p. 79)*
7. La Posta Malbec *(p. 70)*
8. Bogle Cabernet Sauvignon *(p. 42)*
9. Newton Napa Valley Claret *(p. 82)*
10. Yalumba Patchwork Shiraz *(p. 106)*

Top 10 Sweet

1. Dr. Loosen Riesling *(p. 190)*
2. Hermann J. Wiemer Dry Riesling *(p. 191)*
3. Candoni Moscato *(p. 126)*
4. Brandborg Gewürztraminer *(p. 176)*
5. Pacific Rim Sweet Riesling *(p. 195)*
6. Chateau Ste. Michelle Eroica Riesling *(p. 189)*
7. Brokenwood Semillon *(p. 223)*
8. Contra' Soarda Vespaiolo *(p. 229)*
9. Leasingham Magnus Riesling *(p. 192)*
10. Leeuwin Estate Art Series Riesling *(p. 193)*

Special Occasions

All the wines featured in this book are perfect for a party or a gift, and will not break the bank. Here are my wine recommendations for some specific events.

A summer beach party: Pacific Rim Dry Riesling, Cloudline Pinor Noir, J Wine Pinot Gris, Innocent Bystander Pinot Noir, Veramonte Sauvignon Blanc Reserva, Bodegas Mugas.

Thanksgiving dinner: Rayun Syrah Chile, Andezon Cotes du Rhone Villages La Granacha Signargues, Las Rocas de San Alegandro, Joel Gott Zinfandel.

Christmas dinner: Barbera d'Asti Berrro Pico Maccario, Veramonte Primus Chile, Chateau Ste. Michelle Cabernet Sauvignon, Seven Deadly Sins Zinfandel.

Cocktail party: Box-O-Birds Sauvignon Blanc, Paul et Jean-Marc Pastou Sancerre, Yalumba Eden Valley Chardonnay, Frei Bros Merlot, Ravenswood Zinfandel, Catena Malbec.

Housewarming party: Crios Malbec, Shoofly Shiraz, Ménage à Trois Red Table Wine, Kim Crawford Marlborough Sauvignon Blanc, Trevor Jones Chardonnay, Louis Jadot Pouilly-Fuissé.

Memorial Day: Napa Cellars Zinfandel, Fess Parker Syrah, Rodney Strong Zinfandel, Babich Unoaked Chardonnay, Domaine de la Petite Cassagne, Oyster Bay Sauvignon Blanc.

Labor Day: La Posta Malbec, Finnegan's Lake Cabernet Sauvignon, d'Arenberg Laughing Magpie, Bonterra Organic Riesling, Erath Pinot Griogio, Arrogant Frog Chardonnay Viognier.

Potluck dinner: Wyatt Cabernet Sauvignon, Dr. Loosen Riesling, Casa Lapostolle Cuvee Alexandre Merlot, Newton Claret, Sterling Chardonnay, Cancannon Chardonnay.

Night by the fireplace: Pulenta Estate Malbec La Flor, Napa Cellars Cabernet Sauvignon, Kendall-Jackson Vintner's Reserve Cabernet Savignon, Louis Jadot Macon Villages Chardonnay, Santa Barbara Chardonnay.

Special gift: Innocent Bystander Pinot Noir, Vinum Cellars PETS, Bodega Catena Zapata Malbec, Pacific Rim Organic Riesling, Adelsheim Chardonnay, Crios Torrontes.

Glossary

Acid: One description for tasting of wine, sometimes described as sour or tart.

Acidity: All wines naturally contain acid and people often use this term to talk about the taste of wine. It should be properly balanced with fruit and other components. Sufficient acidity gives wine liveliness and crispness. It's critical for wines to age and gives wine thirst-quenching qualities.

Aftertaste: Exactly what it sounds like. The aroma and taste that linger in your mouth and nose after the wine has been swallowed

Appellation: You will find this term on labels. It applies to the specific geographic area the wine comes from.

Aroma: Fancy word for the smell of wine.

Breathing: Technical term is aerating. Opening a bottle exposes the wine to air that can help it develop and mellow, especially red wine.

Balance: A description of wine's components and the equality of the tastes: fruit, acidity, tannins, and alcohol.

Big: Another term for full-bodied, strong taste, and smell

Body: The weight and texture of a wine.

Bottle Aging: Some refer to as aging of wine, which is the process of storing wine in a bottle to help mature and refine its flavors. Wines under $20 are usually ready to drink and do not need to be aged.

Buttery: Usually does not mean the wine tastes exactly like butter, but has the buttery smells and texture. This description is used more with white wines than reds.

BYOB: Bring Your Own Bottle! (My favorite for restaurants—you save a ton of money and can drink what you like!)

Cab: Nickname for Cabernet Sauvignon.

Cabernet: Another nickname for Cabernet Sauvignon.

Chablis: The northernmost wine district of the Burgundy region in France.

Character: The combination of a wine's features that make it unique from others.

Chewy: A description used to describe wines that are unusual in thickness of texture or tannins. Mainly used to describe heavier, full-bodied red wine.

CDR: Stands for Côtes du Rhône.

Complex: I find this term confusing but wine aficionados use it to describe wine with a lot of different flavors and smells. Complexity is good.

Cork: Of course the cork is used to seal the bottle, but the term can also be used to describe a wine that is not good. Usually there is something wrong with the taste, an unpleasant smell. Some people use the term "corked" or corky."

Crisp: Fresh, brisk character, usually associated with the acidity of white wine. I love crisp wine on a hot summer evening.

Decanting: It is a fancy word for pouring wine from its bottle into another container. This allows the wine to breather and is also the best way to separate wine from sediment. Usually done for older wines and is a personal choice for wines under $20.

Delicate: A wine that is light in texture with some flavor, usually light-bodied wines.

Dry: Opposite of sweet, by definition a dry wine has little or no residual sugar left following the fermentation process.

Dull: A term used to describe lack of flavor or zest.

Earthy: A more natural smell, some describe a floral aroma, or flavor reminiscent of earth.

Elegant: A description used for the overall feeling of the wine, usually when the flavor, quality, and style are in balance.

Finish: Aftertaste in mouth—you want the flavor to linger.

Firm: When the wine's structures are tightly wound together, and it also implies the wine has quite a bit of flavor and structure.

Floral: A term used to describe a smell similar to flowers, usually in a Riesling.

Flute: Special tall and slender glass for sparkling wines.

Fortified Wine: Wines with alcohol added: Port, Sherry, Madeira and Marsala are the major categories of fortified wines.

Fresh: Usually used to describe white or rosé wine with a good balance between alcohol and acidity, but may be used for young red wines.

Fruit: One of the common tastes in wines that imitate the flavors and smells of other fruits.

Fruity: Used to describe fruit flavors and smells in wine

Full-bodied: A term used to describe a wine with a lot of flavor, alcohol, and thickness that give a mouth-filling impression.

Green: Description used for a young wine that needs to mature in order to balance out its acidity.

Grenache: A grape used in wine, primarily in Cotes du Rhone.

Harmonious: Used when all the wine elements—fruit, alcohol, acidity, and tannins—are in balance.

Harsh: Rough, biting character from excessive tannin and/or acid. Excessive tannin or acid may be prominent due to a lack of fruit.

Honest: A relatively flawless but simple wine.

Light: Refers to a wine that is light in alcohol and/or texture and weight in the mouth. Some may feel that light wine is weak but others prefer the flavor, as in a Pinot Noir or a Burgundy.

Magnum: A 1,500-milliliter bottle.

Malbec: a red grape from Argentina.

Mature: Ready-to-drink, fully developed wine. Maturing will vary depending on the wine. Most of the wines in this book are "ready to drink."

Meaty: A wine with a chewy, fruity, full, and firm texture. Usually used to describe Cabernets and Zinfandels.

Mellow: Used to describe a low-acid wine, one that's light, soft and easy to drink.

Meritage: California wine producers invented this term to indicate a high-quality wine blended from Bordeaux varieties.

Merlot: A red grape, very popular.

Napa Valley: Wine region in Northern California.

Nutty: A nut-like smell and flavor usually found in white wines.

Oak: Smell and taste, rather vanilla-like.

Pale: With less color then similar type wines.

Petite Sirah: A grape mainly produced in California.

Pinot Grigio: A white-wine grape, also known as Pinot Gris.

Pinot Noir: A red grape of California and Burgundy, known for its light- and medium-bodied wines.

Pouilly-Fuissé: A popular French white wine, made from Chardonnay grapes.

Region: A large subdivision of wine production.

Reserve: A term used to help market wine, with no legal definition in the United States. It is meant to imply that a wine may be aged longer.

Rich: Used to describe wine that has a lot of flavor, body, and aroma.

Riesling: white wine grape that is best known from Germany, Austria, and Alsace.

Rioja: A wine region in Northern Spain.

Robust: Full-bodied, full-flavored, some may say heavy in taste.

Rosé: Pink-colored wine.

Sauvignon Blanc: A lighter wine than Riesling and Chardonnay and an excellent warm-weather wine with food.

Sediment: Debris found at the bottom of a bottle of red wine, which comes from the wine itself.

Shiraz: A red-wine grape; also known as Syrah.

Simple: Often applied to inexpensive wines. (In my opinion, at this price point, it is not a negative statement.)

Smoky: A smell often associated with Sauvignon Blanc and Pinot Noir.

Smooth: A well-balanced wine that is usually light in tannins and acidity.

Sonoma Valley: Region in Northern California where many diverse wines are produced.

Spicy: Wines that have the smell and taste of spices such as pepper, mint, cinnamon, etc.

Sweet: Wines that taste like they have sugar, which could come from the grape not being converted to alcohol. Dry wines may smell sweet from their combinations of fruit and ripeness. (I prefer dry wine but many people like the taste of sweet wine.)

Syrah: A red grape, known as Shiraz in Australia and South Africa.

Tannin: A natural component found in different degrees in the skins, seeds, and stems of grapes, as well as oak barrels. It is most prominent in red wines, where it creates a dry sensation in young reds and usually softens with age.

Thin: My basic description for tasting like water, but professionals say insufficient body, flavor, and color.

Tobacco: A smell that is usually more prominent in older wines. Lovers of Bordeaux look for this aroma.

Tuscany: One of the major wine regions of Italy.

Vin: French for wine.

Vintage: The year of the harvest of the grapes or the date on the bottle.

Vino: Italian for wine.

Viognier: A white grape, usually found in the Rhône Valley, with fruit-like flavors.

Zinfandel: A red grape that thrives in California. A white Zinfandel is made from red-wine Zinfandel grapes.

Wine Index

Resources

Web sites I found helpful for shopping and used for research:

www.andreawine.com — General knowledge

www.bevnetwork.com — General knowledge

www.palmbay.com — Definitions

www.ste-michelle.com — Wine pairings

www.snooth.com — Wine shopping, blogs, tips

www.zachys.com — Source of wine, both at auction and retail

www.wine.com — Buy and general knowledge

www.wine-searcher.com — Compare prices

www.winecurmudgeon.com — Great blog

www.wineloverspage.com — Great blog and general knowledge

www.wine-lovers-page.com/lexicon — Wine pronunciation

www.anotherwineblog.com — A bit advanced but helpful

www.epicurious.com — Food recipes and wine pairings

www.foodandwine.com — Upscale but great

Bibliography

Books

The Only Wine Book You'll Ever Need, Danny May, Adams Media, 2004

The Everything Wine Book, Barbara Nowak and Beverly Wichman, Adams Media, 2005

The Wine Trials 2010, Robin Goldstein and Alexis Herschkowitsch, Fearless Critic Media, 2009

The Worlds Best Value Under $25, Robert Parker, Simon and Schuster, 2009

The Wine Bible, Karen MacNeil, Workman Publishing Co., 2001

Good, Better, Best Wines: A No-Nonsense Guide to Popular Wines, Carolyn Evans Hammond, Alpha, 2010

Windows on The World — Complete Wine Course, Kevin Zraly, Sterling, 2008

Food Pairing Icons

 Meat
   (Beef, lamb, roasts, pork chops, meatloaf)

 Poultry
   (Chicken, turkey, duck)

 Casual foods
   (Hamburgers, hot dogs, chili, pizza)

 Fish and seafood

 Asian cuisine

 Spicy foods

 Cheese

 Salads

 Grilled foods
   (Meats, vegetables, veggie burgers)

 Fruits and Nuts

 Italian and Mediterranean cuisine

Cheers! Salute! L'Chaim! Kampai! Oogy wawa! A Votre Sante!